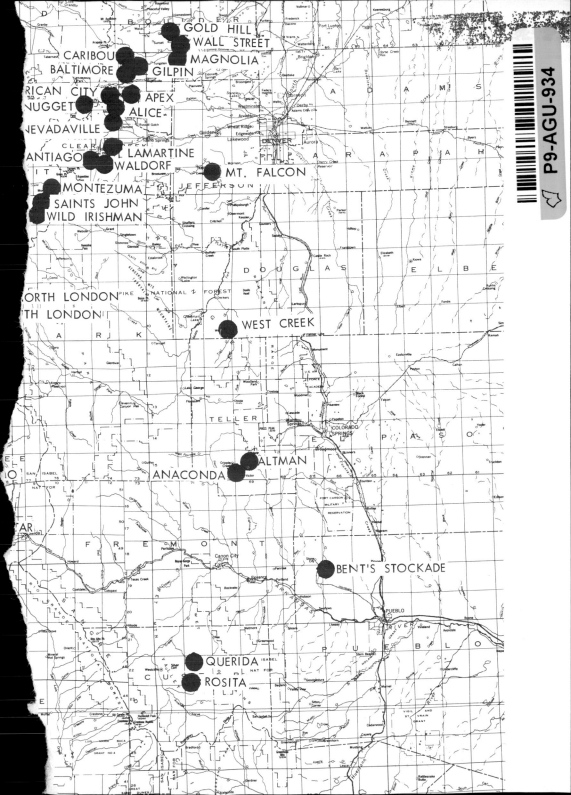

JEEP TRAILS
TO
COLORADO GHOST TOWNS

JEEP TRAILS
to
COLORADO GHOST TOWNS

By
ROBERT L. BROWN

ILLUSTRATED WITH PHOTOGRAPHS

THE CAXTON PRINTERS, LTD.
CALDWELL, IDAHO
1988

First printing, July 1963
Second printing, October 1963
Third printing, December 1964
Fourth printing, July 1966
Fifth printing, July 1968
Sixth printing, July 1969
Seventh printing, January 1972
Eighth printing, June 1973
Ninth printing, July 1976
Tenth printing, September 1978
Eleventh printing, March 1981
Twelfth printing, October 1983
Thirteenth printing, November 1985
Fourteenth printing, March 1988

Library of Congress Catalog Card No. 63-7443

International Standard Book Number 0-87004-021-9

Printed and bound in the United States of America
149027

For
EVELYN, DIANA
and
MARSHALL

ACKNOWLEDGMENTS

IN PREPARING reference materials for this book, a large number of persons, institutions, and sources are deserving of mention for assistance rendered.

First, a special word of thanks goes to Mr. Glenn H. Johnson, Jr., librarian of our State Historical Society, and his fine staff, particularly Mrs. Velma Churchill and Mrs. Laura Ekstrom, for extracting quantities of primary source materials from their files. Next, for at least a like quantity of assistance in the Western History Collection of the Denver Public Library, my thanks to Mrs. Alys Freeze and her staff, especially Opal Harber and James Davis.

For help in reaching and identifying townsites and for their companionship on long trips, a word of particular gratitude is due my wife Evelyn, our two children, Diana and Marshall, and three good friends, Dr. Gerald G. Coon, Jack L. Morison, and J. G. (Pete) Heiney, who often accompanied me in my own Jeep and have many times taken me with them in theirs.

Mr. Charles Parker and Dr. John C. Johnson, of Denver; Mrs. Leland Sharp, of Montezuma; and others with whom I have corresponded and talked have been most generous with their time and information. Francis B. Rizzari rendered invaluable assistance by proofreading the final manuscript and pointing out errors and oversights. Mrs. Evelyn Brown, Miss Shirley Goss, and Miss Dona Newell labored tirelessly through the typing and necessary retyping.

Two excellent reference books were of special value.

First, *Stampede to Timberline,* by Muriel S. Wolle, a handsome and lovingly written volume which belongs on the shelf of every lover of Colorado yesterdays. Second, *A Guide to the Colorado Ghost Towns and Mining Camps,* by Perry Eberhart, is a nearly all-inclusive survey of the State's hundreds of abandoned camps.

Finally, the following references, in alphabetical order, were consulted in my research and proved most helpful: the *Canon City Record* for September 11, 1919, and the *Canon City Mining Gazette* of August 23, 1882; the *Central City Daily Register* of July 21, 1876; the *Colorado Magazine,* November, 1940, and January, 1956; the *Colorado Miner* (Georgetown), published on March 10, 1870, and July 3, 1880; the *Colorado Mining Directory* of 1883; the *Colorado Springs Sunday Gazette and Telegraph* of October 10, 1937; the August, 1954, edition of *Colorado Wonderland Magazine;* George A. Crofutt's *Grip-Sack Guide of Colorado,* published in 1881; the February 27, 1901, issue of the *Denver Republican* and the August 14, 1881, number of the *Denver Tribune;* the *Elk Mountain Pilot* of February 6, 1936; the *Gilpin County Observer* for October 10, 1911; the *Grand Junction Daily Sentinel,* August 16, 1937, edition; the *Gunnison Daily Review* of April 10, 1882, the *Gunnison Democrat* published on February 13, 1881, and the *Gunnison News Champion* of July 20, 1939; C. W. Hurd's pamphlet, *Bent's Stockade Hidden in the Hills;* the *Idaho Springs News* of June 5, 1896; the *Leadville Herald Democrat,* 1922; the *Rocky Mountain News* for the following dates: November 7, 1861; December 14, 1871; October 24, 1878; June 15, October 12, and October 28, 1879; October 5 and December 21, 1880; January 11, 1881; April 3 and December 4, 1882; April 7 and 18, and September 18, 1883; July 12, 1914; September 3, 1919; and January 14, 1934; the *Silver World* (Lake City) for July 27, 1878; the *Silverton Standard* for August 2, 1937, and December

22, 1939; and the *Technical World Magazine,* published on March 7, 1912.

Finally, I suppose a few words of posthumous praise should be given to Ulysses S. Grant for providing good copy by visiting such a multiplicity of Colorado mining camps. Perhaps some day we shall have a volume devoted to Colorado boom towns not toured by the ex-President, ex-General.

R. L. B.

§

INTRODUCTION

DURING the last two decades we have witnessed a hopeful upsurge of interest in Colorado history, particularly as it has been reflected in an awareness of the important part played by the mining period in the overall development of the Centennial State. Further evidence of this concern became statistically apparent during the summer of 1959 when, for a period of six weeks, an electronic brain developed by the International Business Machines Corporation was placed in our Statehouse as a part of the Rush to the Rockies Centennial observation of the original Pikes Peak gold rush. Interested persons could feed any of fifteen hundred selected questions into the device. In the time it was there, a total of 31,789 questions was submitted. Of these, the greatest number for a single subject was 2,502 requests for information about Colorado's ghost towns. The second largest number included 156 inquiries about Colonel W. F. (Buffalo Bill) Cody.

Today, whenever we take the family sedan over the vast network of well-paved highways that lace through the Colorado Rockies, we still see evidences of mining on every side in the form of abandoned shaft houses, occasional clusters of log cabins around a prospect hole, the tremendous hulking shells that were once gravity or stamp mills, and the innumerable old ore-wagon and toll roads that lead off into the high country where a majority of the true ghost towns are situated. It doesn't take a graduate geologist to realize that gold and silver do not often occur in paying quantities within the flat plains country where our larger population centers are found today. Consequently, most of the towns that were established during the mining period were situated off the twentieth-century beaten track, usually high in the mountains in places not shown on contemporary maps, and often in the most inaccessible parts of the state. To revisit these locations where our early Colorado history was written often requires considerable research and sometimes physical labor because most of the ore-wagon roads and pack-mule trails that connected these settlements with the outside world are now overgrown and have seen little or no maintenance since the turn of the present century.

Determining the location of these trails usually involves detailed study and pencil sketching of older maps found in the archives of our State Historical Society, the Western History Collection of the Denver Public Library, or personal interviews with the all too rapidly decreasing number of older persons who actually lived in these towns during the boom days. The next step is to correlate the map with known landmarks to establish the point at which the old trail began, and from there you are on your own. Often you will not see another human being for days at a time. It almost goes without saying that extra cans of gas and a sleeping bag and portable icebox for food are essential parts of the gear to be stashed in your Jeep. Almost as necessary are copies of two superb books on Colorado ghost towns: *Stampede to Timberline*, by Muriel Sibell Wolle, of Boulder, and *A Guide to the Colorado Ghost Towns and Mining Camps*, by Perry Eberhart.

It is not the purpose of this volume to resurvey completely the list of ghost camps, or to rehash the work that has already been so capably done. Instead, it is the author's hope to bring forth some new material about a few selected towns that still offer enough to be seen and studied by the serious observer. In addition, specific and detailed instructions for reaching each town have been included in the text, together with a description of what was there and which things still remain at the site. I have also included at least one of my own contemporary photographs of each and every town described for purposes of record, identification, and comparison. The ghost towns chosen for inclusion here have been picked for some special reason from a wide selection of possible choices because of some particular aspect of their development, appearance, locale, or subsequent history, or for some other reason that makes them outstanding among other towns of similar type.

For my purposes as a teacher of Colorado history it has been found valuable to categorize ghost towns under four classifications: First, of course, and most obvious, is the town that has completely disappeared and is now nonexistent except for a handful of foundations on some remote hillside where nature is in the process of reclaiming its own. Only for the sake of objectivity are a few such towns included here since there is little to be seen at such places and the re-creation of such a town's boom days must be left largely to the imagination. Second, there are the ghost towns where a few or many of the original buildings still line the underbrush-filled streets. Such places may have anything from a few roofless log cabins with abandoned, crumbling mines or mills on nearby hillsides, to towns where several complete streets remain with most of the original buildings still in place. Such towns exist by the hundreds in most of our Western states. From among these I have tried to select a large number of the most interesting, best-preserved but often remote and little-known ghost camps. I do not include such obvious though important settlements as Leadville, Central City, Telluride, Georgetown, Cripple Creek, Fairplay, or Silverton since these and other like communities survived the final blow that was struck when the bottom fell out of the world's silver market in 1893, leaving many communities with no sound basis for existence. The story of such towns has already been recorded, and detailed social history is not my purpose here. Most of these towns now have a permanent population and depend on sources other than mining for their present welfare. To qualify as a real ghost, a town should have been a mining community, founded on the extraction of gold and silver, that has seen much better times and whose streets now hear only the hollow echoes of Memory's tread. Again, for the purpose of objectivity, only two towns that are still occupied have been included here.

Third in my grouping are those pioneer gold and silver camps that died and were abandoned but have since undergone a transformation or rebirth in terms of summer people who have acquired the property through back taxes or other means and who have restored the old cabins for use as cottages or summer homes during a part of each year. A few such towns, represented by Baltimore or American City, are included in this book.

The fourth and last category includes those numerous small camps that grew up around a single mine. Usually these minute settlements were fairly remote and consisted of from three to a dozen or so cabins clustered around the shaft of the only mine. Examples of these would be Santiago and the settlement at the Wild Irishman Mine. To call these "towns" is certainly a misnomer since formal incorporation simply was not a part of the owner's plan and many of them did not include even a primitive post office, though a few did. If additional strikes were made nearby, the influx of population often made a more formal political status mandatory. Such a change would remove them from this category. Many towns began around a single mine and subsequently grew to be much larger.

For the sake of objectivity and ease of reference, all towns included in this volume are listed alphabetically rather than being grouped by geographical or chronological areas. As an added source of reference and convenience to the reader who will be visiting these towns, a brief section has been included at the end of each chapter in which the towns have been grouped by areas.

The most difficult problems encountered in preparing this volume were in the areas of mine production and population statistics. These figures vary widely from source to source. Two examples will suffice. For one of the towns, I found peak population figures that ranged from one hundred and seventy-five to six thousand, with plenty of positively stated guesses in the midrange. In this case the matter was settled by a look at the tiny valley which, with all attendant gulches, could not have held six thousand people. Second, a total mine production figure of $2,000,000 was given for the Bassick Mine in what I have usually regarded as a reliable source. A few lines below this was a statement pegging average production at $200,000 per month. This would limit its life to only ten months and both the Bassick and Querida lasted longer than that. For all such unresolved statements and figures that may have eluded the careful checking, and for any other errors, real or imagined, that may vary with what the reader has seen or heard, the author apologizes in advance.

In conclusion, by way of providing a background against which this book should be read, a few observations are appropriate about conditions indigenous to the Colorado mining period generally and to the founding of these towns specifically.

First to come in the long list of pioneers was the sturdy prospector who, before a trail had been blazed for his guidance, by pick and shovel defied the mountain barriers, tangled thickets, and menacing snowbanks, braving natural dangers as he pushed on to make his discovery. The factor of distance lends a power of enchantment to a miner; he is always ready to follow any will-o'-the-wisp that happens to present an attractive story of rich mines found in some inaccessible country. Next comes the real or alleged discovery and, inevitably, somehow, the secret leaks out. In

1859 and 1860, Colorado mining was dominated by old Californians and Georgians who had already been through the gold excitement in both those locations. Some of them decided it was easier to work Eastern settlers than Colorado's refractory ores and, as a result, the territory became over-run with a race of pseudoscientists who claimed to have perfected processes suitable for the peculiar requirements of local refining.

Next came a boom with placer mining and great hordes of people made the arduous one-hundred-day trip from the Mississippi River to the new Pikes Peak frontier. The economic foundations of the frontier were not firm and depended on new capital from sales of the better mines or from the life savings of the incoming migrants. In this new life on the Colorado frontier there was a lack of conventional customs and institutions. This deprivation resulted in substitute behavior which sometimes caused increased sexual tensions among the more mobile and far more political participation than at home.

The unity of the family was broken in these settlements which were almost exclusively male at first. The result was that they did not feel the restraint of socially defined rules, resulting in involvement with conflict situations due to failure to establish satisfactory social relationships. One author has stated that an uncomfortably large number of the argonauts who arrived after 1865 were the misfits, the ne'er-do-wells, and the first to be unemployed in the depression that followed the Civil War. Some were psychopathic personalities, hence possibly we can explain the presence in Colorado folklore of the several erratic "characters," such as Harry Orchard, Alfred Packer, and others.

Since those families that were most mobile were also the most likely to leave, it is not particularly surprising to note that 60 per cent of all those who came to Colorado during the mining period left by 1870.

The final development phase could take one of the two

following forms: First, if the ore had been sufficiently rich to warrant rebuilding the town after its inevitable fire, then the richest claims were usually sold to outside or absentee capital and the community became a permanent fixture on the Colorado scene. Second, if the reverse were true and a few struck it rich and departed while the hopes of many died without fulfillment, then the area became a ghost town.

Today the eroded, crumbling foundations, the sagging log cabins, and the still-raw scars of yellowed tailing dumps remain to remind those who care to see of the many mining towns which once flourished deep within the mighty ranges of Colorado's majestic Rockies. To recount some of the memories of a few such towns that died in their infancy is the purpose of this book.

Each chapter in this book ends with detailed instructions that were accurate when the site was last visited. However, changes do occur. New trails can by-pass a town, as at Roses Cabin. Fences or gates may appear across former access routes; or, an entire town, like Romley, may be razed or burned.

R. L. B.

CONTENTS

ILLUSTRATIONS

ILLUSTRATIONS   23

JEEP TRAILS
TO
COLORADO GHOST TOWNS

1.

ALICE

You DON'T need a four-wheel-drive vehicle to reach Alice; even the newer cars will make it. While driving west out of Idaho Springs, on U.S. 6 and 40, watch for State Highway 285, on your right, a good graded road that leads all the way up to this small community. It leaves the highway a few miles beyond Idaho Springs and is marked by a sign directing you to St. Mary's Glacier. Several miles up this road are two cabins beside the road on your right. Barely beyond them a side road forks sharply to the left. This is Alice, with its several log cabins nestled among the trees. If this latter road to the left is followed up through Alice you will come to the tremendous Alice Glory Hole, a bit smaller than the one behind Central City atop Quartz Hill but still representative of a sizable undertaking. This one measures about a hundred feet or so across and is said to be fifty feet deep.

Placer gold deposits were worked with hydraulic equipment here as early as 1881, stripping away the top from several acres of land at a time. The town derived its name from the nearby Alice Mine, which in turn was named by its proprietor, a man named Taylor, for his wife Alice. It continued to produce not only gold but smaller quantities of both silver and lead for nearly two decades, finally closing down in 1899.

As you approach the town from the Fall River side, the scarred and yellowing evidence of the exhaustive strip mining can still be seen where the several acres of barren and unproductive terrain lead right up to the evergreens. For a time a large stamp mill operated here to isolate the gold from the stripped-off topsoil; but as the character of the deposits changed, it fell into disuse.

In recent years, Alice has managed a second lease on life with the renovation of several of the better preserved old cabins into summer homes. Old wagon wheels, gardens, flower boxes, and splashes of gaily colored trim are visible here and there among the evergreens that nearly succeed in secreting the structures in their semi-isolation.

As a schoolteacher I shall never forget the story of Alice. Instructional facilities for the settlement were surprisingly adequate. At the far side of one of the few cleared areas in the town stands quite a large white frame school building, architecturally unmistakable in its purpose, built in the unimaginative style of hundreds of its contemporaries in rural Colorado. The story is told that when the town folded in 1899 and the mines played out, the population moved out in a great rush to seek greener pastures elsewhere. It so happened that the exodus took place between paydays and the last teacher was never paid.

In later years a few families did return to live at Alice for varying periods of time in the present century, but the school was never reopened. A school bus took the children down to Idaho Springs and only an occasional bad storm caused them to miss a trip up the hill. Although the cabins beside the Fall River road had collapsed by 1980, the school and most of the other structures remain as described.

---

* In this same area see also Ninety Four.

View from the Glory Hole, looking down on the town of Alice

The school and a cabin at Alice

The intersection and cabins at Alice

2.

ALTA

Alta was an active mining camp, but it never actually became a town. Its economy was based primarily on the Gold King Mine, discovered in the 1870's and worked through the eighties. Alta was basically a one-mine camp. Through the 1890's it continued to produce gold, silver, lead, and copper. The property was acquired in 1904 by the Four Metals Company of Milwaukee and was worked erratically by them until 1917. The School of Mines was involved in a student strike in 1917 and one of the students from the school, a Mr. Russell J. Parker, sampled the ore and took an option at Alta for the Belmont and Tonopah Mining Company. Mr. John Wagner, a bachelor, operated the camp for Belmont-Tonopah, later Belmont-Wagner. The camp was dormant from 1924 to 1938, when it was purchased by H. F. Klock, who operated it until his death in 1945. His widow remarried and still lives in Denver.

After Klock's death, the mining camp reverted back, once more, to John Wagner. On his deathbed, Wagner married his housekeeper of many years. Mrs. Wagner lived in Montrose, but her condition precluded accepting offers for the camp for some time. It apparently is still a valuable mining property and, at this writing, it has just been sold again.

The town contains several cabins, a large boardinghouse, school, tram operator's office, and a number of twentieth-century houses. There was never a church at Alta. The camp contains the portal to the Black Hawk tunnel which reaches back over nine thousand feet to the St. Louis and Alta veins. The mines have produced between fifteen and twenty millions of dollars.

There were three mills at Alta, all of which have since burned. The last one burned in 1945 while seven men were underground. The superintendent, whose son was with the men beneath the surface, ordered the portal to be dynamited, thereby cutting off the draft and stopping the fire.

Today, the camp is deserted, but with the recent sale, it possibly faces a revival. The camp at Alta is not shown on most maps. Only one map that I've ever discovered reveals its location. The surest way to find it is to go up Prospector's Gulch and over Boomerang Hill on a poor dirt road that turns south from State Highway 145 about a mile west of Telluride. The road twists and climbs very steeply, up through groves of some of the biggest aspen trees I've ever seen. There are several intersections with other trails, but if you follow the well-worn ones, you'll reach Alta.

A second route involves following State Highway 145 to New Ophir, then doubling back north on the dirt road to your right which climbs steeply for about ten miles to Alta. This one, unlike the route from Telluride, can be made in a conventional car. A third way involves crossing Ophir Pass, a really thrilling Jeep road that cuts off to the west from the Million Dollar Highway just a few miles north of Silverton at Burro Bridge. Don't try this one in your family sedan since much of it on the west side is a narrow ledge cut from slide-rock.

Ophir Pass was originally opened as a toll road in 1881. It was reopened recently as an exciting Jeep road across the divide. Dropping down from the top on the western slope, the vast and beautiful San Miguel Valley may be seen spread out below you with Old Ophir nestled like a jewel in the center. Follow the rocky ledge down and through both of the Ophirs. Beyond New Ophir on State Highway 145, the good dirt road to Telluride, take the first turn to the right which will be the Boomerang Hill road. This will carry you up the long hill to Alta. By the 1980's some of the roofs have buckled and the porch of the boardinghouse was gone, but you will find enough of the original buildings still standing at Alta to make your visit there a very memorable one.

---

* In this same area see also Old Ophir.

Lizard Head Peak dominates the skyline from this point on the outskirts of Alta

Over the hill and around the corner at Alta. These cabins still had some furnishings in them when last seen.

The main square at Alta. The large structure was the boardinghouse

The back side of Pikes Peak dominates the skyline behind Altman, once the highest town in the Cripple Creek district.

3.

ALTMAN

AMONG the towns of the Cripple Creek district, Altman had the pardonable pride of being referred to as the highest incorporated city in the world during the decades of the nineties and the early 1900's. It had a population of 2,500, down to some 800 in 1910. Its altitude is 10,700 feet above sea level.

There were six lodges that met there weekly. One man had an assay office and there were two restaurants, one drugstore, four rooming houses, and nine saloons. Among the latter were the Thirst Parlor, the Mint, the Silver Dollar, and the Monte Carlo. If any Altman resident got thirsty while in other parts of the district, there were fifty additional saloons in Cripple Creek, six at Independence, one at Lawrence, thirty-six at Victor, four at Anaconda, three at Cameron, and four at Goldfield. There were also two shoemakers at Altman as the hobnail boys were considered very rough on shoe leather.

The *Denver Times* on December 9, 1899, reported that Foreman Sheldon and his linemen of the Colorado Telephone Company were running a line through Altman when they were ordered to quit work and were sent to their homes by Thomas Ferroll, mayor. Ferroll was bitterly opposed to having a telephone line run through his town. He told the foreman he should consider himself under arrest and, picking up an axe, he started to tear down the poles but destroyed only two. The company said the mayor could not prevent them from going ahead with the construction of their line, and the next day work was to be resumed. The mayor was obliged to pay for the poles cut down and also the wages of nineteen men for one-half day.

If a follow-up story was ever written, it cannot be found; but the incident was typical of the fever pitch at which life in Altman progressed.

During the Cripple Creek labor war in 1894, Altman was the stronghold of the union members and the notorious battle of Bull Hill was fought around the townsite. The miners were entrenched on the hilltop and they exchanged shots with the duly constituted militia below. This battle, with its several humorous aspects, would have provided a natural vehicle for the talents of Gilbert and Sullivan. The town had not yet been founded at that time.

Altman was formally incorporated in 1896 and named for Sam Altman, a sawmill operator who is said to have owned and operated the first stamp mill in the district.

At the present time a few buildings still stand along what was once the main street. At the upper end of the town a building reputed to have been the city hall contains a large safe, the last vestige of city government at Altman. At the lower end of the street a corner of the foundation of Union Hall is still visible. Atop the hill is the shaft house of the Pharmacist Mine, staked out by two druggists from Colorado Springs who had no knowledge of mining. The most widely told story has it that they threw their hats in the air and filed a claim at the spot where they landed. The Pharmacist Mine was the result. It produced close to a half-million dollars in gold.

Altman is situated in the saddle between the top of Bull Hill and the top of Bull Cliff. It can be seen on the hilltop above Goldfield, and perhaps the easiest way to reach it is from this point. A real maze of roads covers the hillside but, having taken a proper line of sight, it's not difficult to reach Altman. Another route may be followed in from the High Line above the Molly Kathleen Mine. Follow the road on past Winfield and Midway to the narrow crushed-rock road that goes to your right for the last quarter mile up to the top of Bull Hill and Altman. The view of Pikes Peak from the hilltop is one of the finest available anywhere.*

Although most of Altman's structures were still standing in 1980, the road has been closed and permission is needed to enter the town.

---

* In this same area see also Anaconda and West Creek.

Collection of Vern Carlson
This photograph of Altman in its heyday was made from the same angle as the picture on page 35. Altman was never the highest town in the world but was the most elevated in the Cripple Creek district.

LTMAN, CRIPPLE CREEK DISTRICT, HIGHEST INCORPORATED
TOWN IN THE WORLD

4.

AMERICAN CITY

THE LIFE SPAN of American City was a short one. The town was laid out in the late 1890's and the erection of houses here and there began at once. As sawed lumber was scarce and commanded enormous prices, most of the dwellings were built of logs. American City was a part of the Pine Creek mining district which had its headquarters at Apex, located in the mountains a few miles below.

The discovery of gold in the nineties and the influx of Eastern capital gave impetus to the founding of this settlement high in the hills of Gilpin County. A school was started to serve not only American City but also to accommodate youngsters from a few of the surrounding towns as well. One hostelry, the Hotel Del Monte, and a single large mill called the Mascot were erected at the site and the crumbling foundation of the mill may still be seen at the northeast edge of the town.

The Pine Creek district was not a particularly rewarding one and the people enjoyed only a few short years of prosperity before the inevitable decline began. The scenic setting of American City was, in subsequent years, one of its greatest assets. The town itself is built almost in the saddle between California Mountain and Colorado Mountain, with the huge towering mass of James Peak looming up in the distance behind the main street and dominating the wide panorama of mountains that surround the tiny community.

When the rich ore deposits played out, most of our mining camps withered on the vine and are now in the process of being reclaimed by the elements. Not a few have been destroyed or damaged by fire and vandals. A lesser number, including towns like Baltimore, Vicksburg, and American City, have been taken over and their buildings restored for use as summer cabins.

This, however, was not the end of the line for American City. In the autumn of 1911, after lying dormant for nearly a decade, the town underwent a new surge of activity unlike anything that had occurred in any Colorado mining camp up to that time. Down the hill in Central City, the *Gilpin County Observer,* on October 10 of that year, carried the story under the following title: "American City, Taking Motion Pictures."

The summer colony at American City has been augmented with a company of artists connected with the Selig-Polyscope Picture Company of Chicago. Snug Harbor and Columbine Castle are the scene of gay festivities. Lt. C. S. Rippey and wife entertained the entire company at their castle Sunday evening last. Manager J. A. Golden of the Selig Company is there for the purpose of obtaining realistic mountain settings for several biographic plays which are in course of completion. Myrtle Stedman, wife of Marshall Stedman who is an official of the Company and a former resident of the county, is the leading lady. Needless to say that her ability and natural beauty adds greatly to the charm and success of the pictures. Tom Mix, champion horseman, bronco buster, and fancy trick rider, together with his wife, Mrs. Mix [,] who also is an expert horsewoman, are assigned prominent parts in the plays. Mr. Mix is under contract to appear in the Frontier Days celebration at Cheyenne. In the company are Mr. Tom Carrigan, leading man, Mr. William Duncan, second leader, Otis Thayer, character artist. Ed Kull, who takes the pictures and is considered one of the best camera men in the profession, Hook, the famous Mexican trick rider, is one of the big attractions. Altogether, the Company is one of the best in the motion picture line.

This was not the first contact with Colorado for the great Tom Mix. Before he became famous as a Western motion picture star, he worked as a cowboy in the Cripple

Creek area and later as a bartender on the town's famous Bennett Avenue.

To visit what remains of this early community, follow Eureka Street up the hill out of Central City, keeping to your right as you approach the cemetery on top of the hill. Follow this road up and down the rolling hillsides until you reach Apex. About midway along Apex's main street, turn left, cross the stream, and go on up the moderately steep hill that follows White's Gulch to the northwest for about two miles. When you reach the hilltop, from which James Peak is clearly visible across the valley below, you will see a rocky trail leading off to the right. When last seen, this road had a private-property sign posted at its beginning. American City lies up this road about one mile. Permission should be secured before visiting the town since the old cabins have now been converted to summer residences.*

---

* In this same area see also Apex, Nevadaville, and Nugget.

Turret house, post office, and cabins at American City.
James Peak is at the extreme left of the picture.

The two foreground cabins are among the very oldest at American City

5.

ANACONDA

An almost empty valley, situated about halfway between Cripple Creek and Victor on State Highway 67, was the site of the town of Anaconda. Only a few landmarks of this once prosperous community remain to be seen today. At the head of the gulch stands the huge cribbing that holds back the tailings pile of the Mary McKinney Mine, a rich discovery which produced eleven millions in gold. Below it, down in the gulch itself, are the trail that was the main street and the tiny stone and mortar corner from the foundation of the jail.

During the earliest period it was known as Squaw Gulch, named for the decomposed remains of a female aborigine who was disinterred during an early mining operation. Later, it was called Anaconda for the nearby Anaconda Mine. The third of the large producing properties here went by the unlikely name of the Doctor—Jack Pot. A railroad, the Florence and Cripple Creek, once served Anaconda and followed roughly the same grade as the present highway around Raven and Gold Hills. A wagon road was graded out a few yards above it.

This was once the fourth largest town in the Cripple Creek district. Texas Guinan, who later became famous during the twenties in New York and built a career for herself around the greeting "Hello, Sucker," once was the organist at the Sunday school in Anaconda. Judge Melville B. Gerry, the jurist who acquired a measure of fame by his conduct of the noted cannibalism trial in Hinsdale County and the subsequent sentencing of Alfred Packer, in later years served on the bench at Anaconda and at nearby Mound City. One census placed the population at 1,059 permanent residents, with large numbers of tourists swelling the size of the town during good weather. Old photographs show a long row of frame buildings, clustered generally along one main thoroughfare the length of Squaw Gulch. In 1904 a fire started in a meat market and the gulch formed a natural chimney or channel for a wind that came up and spread the fire quickly and efficiently over the entire length of the town. The water supply was poor and the resulting conflagration became so hot that even the telephone poles burned. Both Victor and Cripple Creek sent their own fire departments to assist but the blaze had too good a start and the whole community went up like tinder. Since then the railroad has gone, too, and, at first glance, the valley shows little evidence of ever having supported a town of any size and prominence.*

---

* In this same area see also Anaconda and West Creek.

*The Mary McKinney mine dump on the hillside above Anaconda.
Main Street is at the lower left.*

*The principal street of Anaconda divides the empty expanse of Squaw Gulch
below the Cripple Creek highway.*

6.

ANIMAS FORKS

THERE ARE three possible ways of reaching Animas Forks. The easiest route involves taking State Highway 110 out of Silverton for the twelve miles up through Howardsville, Middleton, and Eureka. This leads directly into Animas Forks. If in doubt at intersections, take the road that follows the river.

The other two routes, although shorter if you are coming from most places on the eastern slope, involve some terrain suitable only for Jeeps. Both these trails begin at Lake City. The second follows the Lake Fork of the Gunnison River out past Lake San Cristobal on State Highway 351, past the Sherman Camp Ground, then up over Cinnamon Pass. From Sherman on, a Jeep is almost a necessity due to steep, rocky inclines, rather sharp climbing turns, and the ever-present rock outcroppings here and there. At the foot of Cinnamon Pass, as you emerge into the valley, to your right, is Animas Forks.

The third, most spectacular route, follows Hensen Creek out of Lake City to the towns of Hensen and Capitol City. From this point either a Jeep or a mule is essential. During the eighties this was the original stagecoach route over Engineer Pass by way of the historic stage station at Rose's Cabin. It was called the Hensen Creek and Uncompahgre toll road. The distance from Lake City was, and still is, twenty-two miles and a fare of three dollars per person was charged for the trip.

The road continues to rise higher and higher until the

Continental Divide with its icy coronet appears clear-cut and glistening against a background of the most intense blue sky. Take a lunch and start early on this one, pausing in the saddle on top of the pass to enjoy what I regard as the most spectacular mountain panorama in the state. Here are several of the fourteen-thousand-foot-high giants of the San Juans, and other great peaks seem insignificant by comparison. If ever there was a spot where it can be said that you're on top of the world, this is it. Majestic Matterhorn and Wetterhorn, massive Engineer and Redcloud, craggy Coxcomb and mighty Uncompahgre peaks—all are within your horizon from the top of Engineer Pass. Below the saddle to your left are the ruins of the once great Frank Hough Mine.

From this point the road forks in three directions; all of them come together again down below. The middle one is the easier grade but the other two offer more breathtaking scenery. Hold onto your hat as the grades are precariously steep in places. At the foot of the pass keep left until you emerge at Animas Forks. The town is built on the giddy slopes overlooking the gulch, where private residences, stores, saloons, quartz mills and reduction works were crowded in, helter-skelter, as if dropped from the clouds. The other two roads, previously mentioned, go down to Mineral Point, the Million Dollar Highway, and Ouray. At Animas Forks the road joins the one from Cinnamon Pass and follows the railroad bed down Animas Canyon to Eureka and beyond to Silverton.

Even this railroad bed is rich in history. Otto Mears, trusted intimate of Chief Ouray and later famed as the pathfinder of the San Juans, built a spur line called the Silverton-Northern Railroad Company up the canyon all the way to Animas Forks. In 1911 Mears ran a special train called the "Columbine Special" from Silverton to Animas Forks. The purpose was to supply large quantities of our state flower for a convention meeting being held in Denver at the time. Periodic stops were made to enable the pickers to gather some 25,000 columbine blooms from the lofty alpine meadows that open out from the several spots along the canyon. Now the rails have been torn out since 1942 and it's a road once more.

Animas Forks is situated near timberline at an elevation of 11,584 feet above sea level in the northern part of San Juan County, at the forks of the Animas River. Prior to 1877, the year in which the townsite was laid out, miners lived in tents while working their claims and finding employment in the nearby mills. There were two smelting and reduction works situated at or near the town. Among the many valuable mines around the Forks were the Iron Cap, the Black Cross, Eclipse, Little Roy, Red Cloud, Big Giant, Columbus, and the huge Gold Prince. The ores were galena and silver-bearing gray copper. The Little Arthur, Hepburn, and Mountain Queen belonged to Chicago capitalists. Two miles below the town, in Burns Gulch, were the Lilly and Golden Eagles lodes.

Animas Forks contained several stores, a hotel, a number of saloons, two assay offices, shops, and a score of buildings. Its population, including near surroundings, approached 1,500. During the eighties a telephone line was completed from Lake City, crossing the Continental Divide near Engineer Pass at an altitude above twelve thousand feet. The Gold Prince mill was located at the south edge of the town and its gigantic foundations are still there. To really appreciate the vastness of this operation you should view the foundation from the first incline going up out of the town on the Cinnamon Pass road, across the river.

Snow depths in the winter often exceeded twenty feet, with catastrophic snowslides roaring down from the several mountainsides that surround the vulnerable little town. Despite this disadvantage, people lived here the year round. The architectural style of the dwellings proves that the residents regarded this as a community of substance and permanence. These are no mere miners' cabins of rude log construction. Instead, the structures were erected from dressed, finished lumber, have shingled roofs, gables, and bay windows that unmistakably reflect the Victorian influence that dominated the more substantial edifices of the period.

The only building in town that defies the otherwise harmonious surroundings is the boxlike jail, just off the south end of the one principal street. Built entirely of two by sixes laid flat, the little jail seems as out of place as a cow on the front porch. To me, the interior is its most thought-provoking feature, with the jailer's office at the front. Directly behind are two cells. In today's world a jail with only two tiny cells would seem surprisingly inadequate for a community the size of Animas Forks. In reality, it appears likely that the residents were probably so busy just trying to keep warm while making a living at this altitude that little time was left for inserting ice picks in other people's tires and other genteel forms of juvenile amusement so popular in today's enlightened society. As of this writing, all the barred windows, including one in the door, are still in place.

North of the jail and on the opposite side of the street stands the most impressive house in the town. It is a large two-story structure with a prominent Taft bay window overlooking the canyon of the Animas River. This old home may be potentially rich in the lore of early Colorado history. For here, according to persistent local rumors that I have been unable to prove or disprove, dwelled the family of Thomas F. Walsh, famed for his discovery of the rich Camp Bird Mine in the Imogene Basin above nearby Ouray. Some say that the Walsh family lived here at the time when Tom Walsh had an option on the nearby Early Bird property. Still another local rumor, that I have been unable to substantiate, has it that Walsh's daughter, Evalyn Walsh McLean, returned to the old home while writing her biography *Father Struck It Rich*. She was, perhaps, better known as the most publicized owner of the fabled and ill-fate ¹ Hope diamond, purchased with money made from Colorado's mines. Tattered remnants of linen-backed wallpaper inside the living room give evidence of an opulent and beautiful way of life.

The old house once provided a most welcome night's shelter for a companion and myself who sought to escape the ravages of a summer storm that overtook us just below the summit of Engineer Pass. The unleashed fury of nature, as manifested in a storm at this altitude, is a never-to-be-forgotten event that must be experienced to be appreciated. To the north of the Walsh homestead stands a smaller, less pretentious but quite necessary structure in mute testimony to the fact that even the rich could not design a plumbing system that would operate satisfactorily in this wild and lonely place where water often freezes at night, even during the summer.

The decline of the Forks began in the nineties and, except for occasional "summer people," sheepherders, and sporadic squatters, the town has been deserted since the mid-1920's.*

In 1980 most of the original buildings, including the Walsh house, were still standing. The road up from Silverton has been much improved.

---

* In this same area see also Eureka, Gladstone, Howardsville, Middleton, Mineral Point, and Rose's Cabin.

Local legend has it that Tom Walsh lived in this house while he had an option on the Early Bird Mine at Animas Forks.

William H. Jackson made this early photograph of Animas Forks

This early photograph shows Animas Forks as a partial tent city. Note the excavation for the Gold Prince Mill in the foreground below the town.

In August of 1965 the author made this photograph of Animas Forks, taken from the same spot as was the picture above.

7.

APEX

DURING the short span of Colorado's history, from the beginning to the present time, there have been two towns in the state that took the name of Apex. The first is entirely gone while much remains to be seen of the second.

Back in the days of the sixties there was a town called Apex behind the hogback, halfway between the sites of Golden and Morrison, at the mouth of Apex Gulch, where a toll road ran through it and up the gulch to Idaho Springs, Central City, and Black Hawk. Indians used to winter there and ride their ponies over the hogback to what is now the Pratt and Rooney ranch on Green Mountain to shoot buffalo. Early legends of Arapahoe and Jefferson territories tell of a party of vigilantes who kidnapped a felon from his cell in Golden and strung him from a tree limb at the mouth of the gulch. Now, nearly a century later, the town is coming to life again with cowboys, Indians, and other assorted phenomena at Magic Mountain, built over the site of old Apex.

The second and more recent of the two Apexes was built near the base of Idaho Hill, about five miles northwest of Central City. It was first platted in 1895, rather late as compared with most of the other Colorado mining communities. Before the end of the year there were about 120 houses along both sides of Pine Creek, and the best was yet to come. The *Idaho Springs News* reported in its issue of June 5, 1896, that:

Last year there were not a hundred houses in the town. Now they number over eight hundred and more are rapidly going up. There are three large lodging homes, two dance halls and several saloons. Crowds of people flock in daily and the stages are unable to haul them all. Many have to stay in Central City overnight and come out in the morning.

Apex became the trading center of the Pine Creek mining district and nearby settlements like Nugget and American City carried on most of their trade and commerce here. In later years, the twenty-two-room Apex Hotel was constructed and it is still in a remarkably good state of preservation. The Pioneer Hall fulfilled a multiplicity of civic needs. It was a school, a general community meeting place, a church for the preacher of whatever denomination happened to be passing through, and a social center and dance hall on Saturday nights. Despite all this activity, it is still standing and remnants of the old stage can still be seen. It may be identified currently by its distinguishing hip roof with a flagpole rising from its center. The town also boasted a general store, three saloons, and a meat market, now gone, which sat between the hotel and Pioneer Hall, a space now occupied by the intersection with the road to American City, up White's Gulch.

A choice of two good routes, both equally passable, will carry the prospective visitor along the road up Pine Creek to Apex. From State Highway 119, just north of Black Hawk, take the first left turn and follow the most used road until you reach Apex. An alternate route, which joins up with the one previously described, takes off from the top of Cemetery Hill behind Central City. Follow the road that is second from your right, up and down over an assortment of hills, until the last extended climb that leads up past the big hotel, adorned with the "Tolin" sign, into Apex.

A fire, about thirty years ago, destroyed the business district of Apex but a surprising number of the original buildings survived and are still there. During the summer months, Apex is anything but a ghost camp since a number of its cabins along Pine Creek, in the town and beyond, are occupied sporadically with summer visitors. There's still a lot to see in Apex and photographers will enjoy the wide panorama of the town, spread out along the gulch, with the massive snow-capped bulk of Mount Evans rising above the main street. The mountain, from across a few valleys, looms up in the far distance.*

By 1980 both the Pioneer Hall and the dance hall were gone, but all others are intact as described.

---

* In this same area see also American City, Nevadaville, and Nugget.

Pioneer Hall (at left) and cabins at Apex in the Pine Creek mining district

Main street at Apex. The road to American City runs between the two buildings at the left.

8.

BALTIMORE

AFTER A long period of dormancy, Baltimore now has a second lease on life and its cabins currently show evidence of habitation.

Pick up State Highway 119 at either Boulder or at the foot of Floyd Hill and drive to Rollinsville. Just north of the bridge, turn west on the good dirt road that goes on to East Portal and Tolland. When last seen, the road that branches left to Baltimore was marked by a battered black and white wooden sign with the town's name on it. Since many of Baltimore's cabins are occupied during the summer and as there is currently some local feeling about Jeeps, it's best to leave your vehicle near the sign and walk the last half mile or so into the town.

The history of Baltimore is extremely obscure. We do know that it was large enough to have supported a small opera house and a hotel. The townsite was, and still is, a particularly pretty one, laid out around the edges of a cleared, rectangular meadow. A large number of small, neat, log-walled cabins are nestled in among the pines along the edges of the clearing. A few structures, including the bar, are now roofless, and a large, two-story frame structure, which was the biggest building in town, is down nearly flat on the ground. This latter has been identified variously as having been both the opera house and the hotel. At least one new twentieth-century home has been added at the far end of the meadow.

In winter, due to heavy mountain snows, Baltimore is

difficult of access but can be entered on snowshoes and does present some unusual picture possibilities. In summer it is well to ask permission before entering the town since it is private property.*

By 1980 the saloon had started to sag, but other buildings are unchanged.

* In this same area see also Caribou and Gilpin.

The well-preserved town of Baltimore, west of Rollinsville

The unbroken snow at Baltimore

9.

THE ORIGINAL BENT'S STOCKADE

AFTER HIS failure at Astoria, Oregon, John Jacob Astor moved east, organized the American Fur Company, and soon monopolized fur trading in the upper Mississippi Valley. After 1822, with St. Louis as a base of operations, trappers entered the Missouri Valley, working their way farther and farther up the river, crushing or consolidating with their competitors. President Zachary Taylor once described their operation in the following manner: "Take the American Fur Company in the aggregate, and they are the greatest scoundrels the world ever knew." Astor retired from the company in 1834, but American Fur remained dominant in the Missouri Valley for another decade.

Between 1826 and 1828 the Bent brothers, Charles and William, while in the employ of the American Fur Company, constructed a stockade on the banks of Turkey Creek in the foothills west of Pueblo. It was first believed to have been erected on the Arkansas between present Pueblo and Canon City. Since that time the earlier error has been corrected by the relentless research of Mr. C. W. Hurd, of Las Animas, who rediscovered and identified the ruins from early descriptions.

Its construction was of the stockade type with high cedar posts or pickets driven into the ground. Purpose of the structure was, of course, to serve as a trading post. Three streams within the radius of a few miles offered good prospects for trapping. Both the northern extension of the Santa

Fe Trail and the Taos Trail were close at hand for outgoing and incoming shipments.

Inside the stockade walls were three houses. Their fireplaces are still visible at the site, with bits of metal and molten glass strewn around them. What remains of the original outer walls can be seen in the row of stumps, none of which is over two feet high now, stretching away in a straight line. Two well-worn ruts enter one of the corners where, presumably, the main gate once hung. The tread is too narrow to have been caused by Jeeps and the hilly terrain has perpetuated the tracks by erosion. Indian artifacts and a skeleton have been found in the last two years, due to the coincidence that this historic spot has been "lost" in the rush of civilization and has not been picked over.

The Bents undoubtedly felt that close proximity to the Indians would prove to be an asset for trading purposes, but it turned out just the opposite. The Utes, who lived in the mountains, were traditional enemies of the Cheyenne and Arapaho of the plains. Unknown to the Bents at the time, their stockade was located in the foothills, a buffer zone or no-man's-land where, by common agreement, the Indians rarely trespassed for fear of encountering their foes. Before the end of 1828 they had decided to abandon the site and had moved on, later constructing the better known Bent's Fort on the Arkansas.

To see the few remaining landmarks, follow State Highway 115 south from Colorado Springs past the Hitchrack Ranch, home of the late Warden Roy Best. Between one and two miles south of the ranch, a dirt thoroughfare known locally as the Lytle Road leaves the pavement to your left or east. This should be followed for fourteen miles, then keep left at the only intersection until you find yourself immediately adjacent to the only landmark in the area, Saddlehorn Butte, recognizable by its shape. At the butte, drive across the bridge and cattle guard to a trail that leaves the road to your right. About a half mile down, the trail divides. Go left for an additional half mile to the stockade.

Although not a ghost town in the ordinary sense, Bent's Stockade represents a very early attempt to extend civilization westward, one of the few that still retains something worth seeing. Since it, too, was abandoned after a promising beginning, it seems to share a common bond with the mining camps of four decades later and is therefore worthy of inclusion here.*

Although the Bent Stockade is still there, the site is now on Fort Carson's artillery range. At present, access is difficult.

---

* In this same area see also Querida and Rosita.

My son Marshall beside a fireplace at Bent's Stockade.
Saddlehorn Butte is across the valley.

Wagon ruts and stockade posts mark the site of the Bent brothers' original
stockade on Turkey Creek.

10.

BURROWS PARK

THE NAME of Burrows Park currently applies both to the high meadowland area as well as to the community that once flourished in it. The park in which the town was located is about five miles in length, but only one-half mile wide. It was founded in 1877 and was nearly always deserted in the winter due to the fact that it was situated at an elevation of 10,700 feet. Three 14,000-foot peaks are nearby. Red Cloud and Sunshine are together just to the north of the town and Handies lies to the southwest. The mines were quite rich here, with several which regularly produced between $100 and $600 per day. Chief among these were the Undine, Napoleon, and the Oneida. Burrows Park, though large in area, was never blessed with great numbers of people. Population of the camp varied between 50 and 200 persons over the years. Most of these people were employed in assay work since, in addition to the above-named mines, there were also several hundred other locations that prospected quite well. About a mile above the town there was a sizable reduction works that utilized jigs to separate valuable minerals from the rock. The park was served by a stagecoach line that followed Post Road No. 77 from Lake City, and the fare was $3.00. The stage also continued on over to Animas Forks and the cost of that hair-raising, ten-mile ride was $1.50 either way.

The 10,700-foot-high Burrows Park meadow is situated above the Lake Fork of the Gunnison River, twenty-one miles west of Lake City. From Lake City, take State Highway 351, turning right at the campground that now occupies the former site of the town of Sherman. Follow this road as it switches back steeply upward until you come to two cabins on your left and the U.S. Forest Service sign identifying this as Burrows Park. In reality, two groups of cabins and mines that you will come to prior to the sign were also a part of the community.

The ride up here from the Lake City side is a particularly scenic one. On my last visit to Burrows Park, it was quite late in the afternoon. As we moved along through this wild, beautiful canyon, with the evening sun bathing mountaintops and valleys in a dreamy, mystic light, the surrounding mountainsides were all aglow with rainbow-tinted flowers. Very few mining camps have been situated in such majestic surroundings. The road goes on beyond the town and crosses Cinnamon Pass at an altitude in excess of thirteen thousand feet before dropping down to the craggy valley of the Animas River on the opposite side of the ridge.

At the upper end of the valley there existed for a time a community that called itself Tellurium. It was a very small camp with a population of only twelve persons who watched the world go by from an elevation of 10,872 feet, near the headwaters of the Lake Fork of the Gunnison River. The town's name represented an expression of hope on the part of the residents that tellurium would be found there. The hope was not realized and the town was deserted. An expensive mill was also left behind in the exodus. Tellurium's location was about a mile beyond the upper end of Burrows Park, or twenty-two miles west of Lake City. It, too, was served by the stagecoach line.*

In 1980 both cabins were still intact in the lower town, but a Forest Service picnic ground now occupies the site of the structures in the upper picture on page 66.

---

* In this same area see also Carson, Sherman, and Whitecross.

These cabins at Burrows Park are now flat on the ground.
The picture was made in August of 1958.

Two more of the widely dispersed cabins that were once a part of
Burrows Park, above Lake City.

11.

CAPITOL CITY

GALENA CITY was the original name given to this beautifully situated but now deserted mining camp located up Hensen Gulch, nine miles west of Lake City in Hinsdale County. Here, on the eastern slope of the San Juan-Uncompahgre Range, at an altitude of 9,480 feet, the road levels off and the canyon widens into a park, majestically cupped by the rugged peaks. At this point the creek is generously terraced with beaver dams, mountain willow, aspen, and evergreen trees which are in the process of reclaiming the townsite. Galena City was founded in the 1870's after silver had been discovered here, and soon there came the inevitable post office plus the usual complement of saloons and log cabins. Mainstays of the city's economy were George Lee's sawmill and his Hensen Creek Smelting Works. It was always one of Colorado's most isolated camps. Ouray was and is sixteen miles away on the other side of the ridge. Stagecoach fare from Lake City was $1.50, or the prospective visitor could ride the twelve-mile stage line in from Animas Forks for $1.75.

When Crofutt visited the camp in its earlier years, he had the following to say of its economic prospects.

Work has demonstrated there are many rich mines and mining prospects near the camp but the owners are sitting and fighting and the smelting works are idle while waiting for something to turn up. In a mining country the dog in the manger policy is well exemplified. The more valuable the mines and property, the more certain they are to be tied up and ruined by quarreling and litigation. Prospects for wealth in any mining camp were seldom richer than in Capitol City and it is to be hoped that the clouds will clear away and great prosperity result.

In many ways the story of Capitol City is inseparable from that of George S. Lee and his dream that failed to materialize.

As Galena City grew, so did George Lee's delusions of grandeur. His driving ambition was to become Colorado's governor and to transform this tiny silver camp in the San Juans into the capital city of the state. The initial step, taken in 1870, was to construct a proper and fitting Victorian mansion. Workmen were imported from various parts of the state and the residence was completed at an estimated cost of one dollar per brick to have them hauled in from distant Pueblo. It contained beautiful living rooms, a large bay window overlooking the lofty peaks beyond Capitol Park, a small theater with an orchestra pit, several bedrooms opening off a long central hall on the second floor, and some say there was also a formal ballroom. Even the stables and outbuildings were of brick construction. It was known locally as the Lee mansion, but Lee himself called it "The Governor's Mansion," and as a final step in the plan he changed the town's name to Capitol City. That was as far as his dream progressed. The price of silver dropped, and the residents despairingly deserted the little town. The Lees held out, defied the odds, and stayed on for a time. As the years passed and they grew older, they returned only in the summer. At last the fine old home was deserted. The east wing, outbuildings, and south side have now fallen away, and souvenir hunters have taken a heavy toll in damages. However, much of the Lees' dilapidated mansion still stands at the side of the road, partly hidden by untended willows, a skeleton of memories and stately old red bricks slowly falling to the ground. Despite this, from its frontage on the Hensen Creek Road, it still appears nearly intact.

Today you can drive to Capitol City, lying in its broad

alpine meadow about nine miles up Hensen Creek from Lake City, on what used to be called Post Road No. 15. The narrow, winding, rocky road is usually passable for most automobiles with a little care, but a Jeep is needed if you plan to go on over Engineer Pass on the road beyond. The first landmark will be the Lee mansion at your left. About twenty-five yards beyond, the road bears left into Capitol Park to reveal several more cabins, including a genuine old false front. The rest of Capitol City is gone.*

All of the Lee mansion disappeared in the 1970's but the saloon is still there.

---

* In this same area see also Mineral Point and Rose's Cabin.

The Lee Mansion or Governor's House at Capitol City. The picture was taken in 1959 – the house is almost gone now.

12.

CARIBOU

THERE ARE several versions of the story concerning the discovery of the rich silver lode near the summit of the range in Boulder County. All have the following points in common. First, Sam Conger was the discoverer in all versions except one, in which credit is given to a man named Martin from Black Hawk. Second, Conger was a man of small stature, a bundle of nerves, who came west with a bull train while searching for adventure. Third, the discovery occurred in 1869 and was named Caribou because of game that Conger and Martin had shot there which resembled the caribou or reindeer. These were most probably elk. Fourth, Conger and Martin dug the original claims that eventually became the rich Caribou Mine.

Beyond these four points, however, the narratives sometimes differ widely. The veracity of any of them would be difficult to establish. The one I have chosen to repeat here has been less widely circulated but, to me, it is by far the most interesting of them all and may or may not be true. Parts of it, at least, probably have some basis in fact.

After his arrival in the new territory, young Sam Conger's attention was frequently drawn to the quantity of shiny silver ornaments worn by the Arapaho Indians. Conger questioned their leader, Bird Chief, at length in an effort to discover the source of the tribe's wealth. The chief, naturally, became suspicious and watchful whenever the young adventurer plied him with questions. While the tribe was staying at a favorite camping spot on middle Boulder Creek,

Conger visited them and, at this time, first suspected the existence of a treasure mountain. From this point on, Bird Chief never again referred to the silver jewelry despite Sam Conger's frequent encouragement. Conger never abandoned the hope that someday he would find the source of tribal wealth, and to this end, he spent days and weeks living in the high ranges while pursuing the search.

An element of romance enters the story at this point with the appearance of the beautiful Arapaho princess, Moaning Dove, daughter of Bird Chief. She had more than a passing interest in Sam Conger who was, surprisingly, always a welcome visitor at her father's tepee. She listened avidly to the incredible stories of the outside world that Conger related. One fine day, while they sat beside a mountain stream, she, at last, promised to lead him to the treasure mountain, and some credit for its discovery must fall to her. At this time she gave Conger directions for reaching the mountain and further agreed to lead him to it herself. The following night, while the tribe slept, Moaning Dove departed stealthily sometime after midnight and made her way under cover of darkness to the high ranges and her rendezvous with Sam Conger. As she emerged from the dark forest, the story has it that her eternally watchful father, Bird Chief, suddenly emerged from the gloom, confronted her, and, without a word, indicated the direction of her retirement. As many a daughter of the twentieth century has since done, under like circumstances, she made her way back to the family tepee. Bird Chief shortly discovered Conger pacing to and fro in the moonlight, and discussed with him the honor of his tribe and the integrity of the human race. Under the circumstances, Conger agreed to respect the tribe's rights and promised to abandon his search for the treasure mountain.

Time passed and much water trickled under the bridge. In the course of human affairs, further demands, and encroachment by the ever-increasing hordes of white settlers resulted in removal of the Arapaho from Colorado. Subsequently, Conger now felt free to pursue his search once more. He had no knowledge of mining or minerals, only Moaning Dove's instructions as he remembered them. After several months of hunting he became aware of the fact that he invariably arrived back on the same mountain, marked by large outcroppings of a strange and beautiful rock. Eight years after the disclosure by Moaning Dove, Conger happened to be in Black Hawk purchasing supplies. He showed samples of the rock to a man named Martin who suspected that it was silver. Together they returned to the mountain, staked a claim which they named the Caribou, later called Caribou Hill.

During the next year the district was overrun with mines and prospectors and a town was founded. Within a few months, it claimed three thousand inhabitants. The first were in tents but, within a short time, many substantial buildings were erected.

Being 9,905 feet above sea level, the camp had snow nine months out of the year, blown by a constant west wind. The community never had less than five saloons among its twenty or so business houses. Caribou also had a good water system, but it was allowed to fall apart and now the only source of water is a drinking trough fed by the flow from a caved-in mine.

The Planter's House and the Sherman House were both hotels noted from coast to coast for their service and meals. Best of the two was the Sherman House, although guests were often forced to leave and enter through upstairs windows during the winter. Drifts would be built up in back of the houses and eventually form one huge snowbank the whole length of the town. Children and grown-ups would slide for one-half mile with a variety of gadgets, principally toboggans, sleds, and go-devils.

Borne by the constant wind, snow would sift through any tiny cracks in the buildings, making some aspects of a year-around home in Caribou something less than desirable.

Twice Caribou was nearly wiped out by fire. The first time, in 1879, a forest fire swept in from the west and forty houses were destroyed before the flames were stopped. The second big blaze was in 1905 and Caribou never recovered completely from that one since silver mining had declined because of the low price and there wasn't much incentive to rebuild.

Caribou was once rebuilt from its own ashes. A boom in the price of silver might cause it to be revived for a second time.

Two epidemics also ravaged the little community. Scarlet fever and diphtheria took a heavy toll. The Caribou cemetery, located about three fourths of a mile north of the town, contains numerous headstones of young children and infants who died during the epidemics. This untended burial ground has returned to weeds and is the bleak resting place of most of Caribou's dead. Nearly all of the markers have been pushed over by the wind, and the weather has worn the inscriptions so that now only about fifteen can be read. Numerous young children, under ten years, died in a smallpox epidemic. Many of them share a common year of death.

Caribou was strictly a mining camp, the principal one in Boulder County. It had a stamp mill and concentrating works. The Caribou, Native Silver, 7-30, and Blue Bird were the chief mines. After the town was established, the Caribou Mine was sold to a Dutch company. The miners wrested twenty million dollars from the region's many claims, but the Caribou itself was the richest of the lot, with a total production of some six or eight millions of dollars. Its wealth was brought into the public eye in 1882 by the spectacular stunt of "paving" the street in Central City with a walk of silver bricks made from Caribou ore. When President U. S. Grant first visited Central City in 1882, he stepped out of his carriage into the Teller House on this same path of silver bricks from the Caribou Mine, laid especially for the occasion.

During its boom period the route used was the ore-wagon trail between Caribou and Cardinal to Nederland, Black Hawk, and then to the mint in Denver. The town was, and is, twenty-two miles west from Boulder by stage post road and twenty-one miles from Central City. From Denver, it was sixty miles. Fare by rail and stage was $7.85.

The present road to Caribou climbs steeply upward toward the west from what is now Nederland. The distance is only eight miles and can be driven easily by car. A Jeep is not essential. If you go there, you'll have to return by the same way you went. At the first branch in the road, turn right around the switchback and, at the next fork, go left. About a mile before you reach Caribou, a few shacks and a mine mark the site of Cardinal, a sinful community populated by the racy elements after they had been run out of the upper town. You will recognize Caribou by two stone buildings at the right of the road with a huge open meadow at the left and another cluster of buildings nearly on the crest of the hill upon which the town was built.

Surrounded by snow, peaks, and timbered ridges, all that remains of this once roaring community near timberline atop Caribou Hill are these few dilapidated buildings, bleached by the weather and pushed into a tired eastward slant by the unceasing winds that are born on the Continental Divide not far to the west. The famous old Todd House, once a Caribou landmark, fell down two winters ago. What remains of it may be seen about twenty yards on the other side of the top of the hill in a small clearing that was once the suburb called Dutch Park.

Visitors to Caribou often wonder about the corduroy road, a section of which can be seen in the boggy area near the town. It was a military project, started by two Army engineers, Gordon and McHenry, during the Mormon war.

No one knows its purpose but probably it was to be a supply route as it extended through Four Mile Canyon to Sunshine, Sugarloaf, and Caribou, where it was abandoned since it was not used much. Today, only a few of the old logs remain.

Very little of Caribou is left today, and there will be progressively less next year and the year after. In addition to silver, geologists have since discovered that the town was built atop a tremendous dike of iron, making this a favorite playground for summer electrical storms. Future prospects for old Caribou would seem very dim indeed.

This, then, has been the fate of the town of which it was once said that so much wealth was taken out of the mines here that Caribou taxes built the Boulder County Courthouse.*

By 1980 the site had changed little, but the cemetery had been vandalized.

---

* In this same area see also Baltimore and Gilpin.

The nearly obliterated remains of Caribou in the high meadow above Nederland

The Todd House, once a prominent hostelry in Dutch Park, a Caribou suburb

13.

CARSON

IF YOU enjoy time spent ferreting out choice nooks and bits of scenery, that are, in a manner of speaking, comparatively as much undiscovered as when Columbus first landed; and if you like a town that has a mystery connected with it, the remote Carson may be heartily recommended on both counts.

You will need a mule, a pair of hiking boots, or a Jeep if you decide to attempt the almost perpendicular climb up to this well-preserved ghost town. Start at Lake City and drive about six miles southwest on State Highway 351 past Lake San Cristobal and follow the Lake Fork of the Gunnison River, which leads into the high country. A small sign, erected on the left side of the road by the U.S. Forest Service, points out the steep, rocky, four-mile trail up Wager Gulch to Carson. The generally hazardous nature of this ore-wagon obstacle course would easily rank it beside the routes to Holy Cross City, or across Williams Pass, as one of the worst Jeep roads in the state. There are streams to ford, soft peat bogs to sink down into, huge boulders and rock outcroppings to be driven across. Yet these very conditions are probably a blessing in disguise since they are very likely the only reasons why Carson remains as a superbly preserved example of a ghost town. About eighteen houses, a hospital, a false-fronted store with shelves and show-cases, a beautifully preserved and bleached waterwheel in the stream, and innumerable nondescript items of mining machinery still mark the townsite.

From the standpoint of history, the earliest discovery was

made by Christopher Carson, who staked out the Bonanza King Mine nearly on top of the divide and about a mile beyond the present town. It was in 1881 that the mining district was organized. Since many towns have been named for the first persons to settle, trap, or mine in a region, it was logical that the incoming argonauts should name the camp that sprang up the following year, in 1882, for Chris Carson. The prime attraction was silver at first and the town was increasingly active throughout the eighties, with its peak development coming in the early nineties. The first trail to serve the region was built up Wager Gulch from west of Lake City. In 1887 a second road was pushed through from Lost Trail Creek west of Creede. The latter name was a prophetic one since the Lost Trail Creek route is now nearly overgrown and currently suitable for little other than hikers or horses.

Early records tell us that the town must have been sizable since its elevation extended from 11,500 to 12,000 feet at the crest of the divide. With this in mind it is not surprising that Carson was all but deserted in winter.

About 150 claims were worked nearby. Chris Carson's Bonanza King continued to be one of the best but its production was exceeded by the St. Jacobs, also located on the ridge above town, which produced in excess of $300,000 in both gold and silver. The silver crash of 1893 was thought to have finished the town but in 1896 gold was discovered and a second lease on life for Carson became a reality.

And here the mystery begins, for about two miles further on up the trail past the town, and situated atop the Continental Divide, are the ruins of another town with several cabins constructed with tremendous logs in the cabin walls. One author states that Carson was a huge place and that its cabins were laid out on both sides of the divide. This would indicate that both settlements were originally a part of Carson.

A second version comes from the local dude ranch oper-

ators who occasionally bring a Jeep load of their guests to
the town. They call the larger, lower town Carson, as does
the Forest Service, whose marker indicates a distance of
four miles which, when checked on two different Jeeps,
takes us only to the lower community. This conclusion
leaves the upper town unnamed.

The third story comes from a Durango prospector who
first began operations here in 1915 and is still mining quite
actively in the area. He maintains that the upper settlement was Carson and that the lower, more complete set
of buildings was called Bachelor Cabins. Nearby is the site
of the Bachelor Mine. The settlement had its own post
office, which was located in the general store. The building is still standing and is the one with the large false front
at the extreme north end of the meadow. Further south
along the left side of the main street is a building that is
currently filled with mining supplies. Originally this was
the mine office. The larger building almost directly behind
it was a boardinghouse at first. Later it was converted to
a community hospital.

If you accept this latter version of the mystery, it will
be easier to understand the remarkably well preserved state
of the fifteen to twenty buildings since the boom of the
Bachelor Mine occurred between 1905 and 1915 and the
construction, therefore, would date from that time. Carson,
on the other hand, being older and on top of the divide
at twelve thousand feet, near Bent Peak, is badly dilapidated.
The logs are bleached from exposure, with no protection,
to the severest elements. Since the town was built atop
a dike of iron, summer electrical storms are particularly
attracted to it. Surprisingly, about six structures are still
standing. Of these, the largest was the hotel. Within it
were the saloon and general store. Another of the buildings
that is still up was a second "general purpose" type containing the boardinghouse and post office. A third edifice
was the office building of the Bonanza King Mine. Look-

ing at this fast-diminishing cluster of cabins, it's easy to believe that the area was deserted in 1893, the year of the miners' first exodus from Carson.

There is some evidence to support each of these stories. The truth, when finally known, will probably be a partial combination of all three. Since it was not unusual in the history of Colorado for a town to move completely, as Red Mountain did, it would seem possible that some truth exists in all of the stories. Probably the older town on top of the ridge was the original Carson which boomed with silver and expired with repeal of the Sherman Silver Purchase Act of 1893. This would explain the discrepancy between early records and the present locations in terms of elevation above sea level.

In 1896, when gold was discovered below the ridge, new buildings were constructed in order to be closer to the Bachelor, a gold property. The name of Carson was adopted since it was in the same area and the former town was now deserted. This would explain the observation that it was built on both sides of the divide and also the Forest Service mileage estimate. It is my own opinion that both towns were Carson. Two towns built around two booms with two different metals at two separate times—but they were close enough together to have gone under the same name. Carson, or Bachelor Cabins—take your choice. It would be a pleasure to hear from someone in possession of sufficient facts to bring the true story into proper focus.*

In 1980 both townsites remained approximately as described, although some cabins are now sagging.

---

* In this same area see also Burrows Park, Sherman, and Whitecross.

The well-preserved, but almost inaccessible lower town of Carson, showing many of the assorted buildings still standing at the site.

Waterwheel and assorted cabins at the lower and later town of Carson, high above the Lake Fork of the Gunnison. Note the stone retaining wall.

The old, original town of Carson, perched atop the Continental Divide high above Lake City. Note the Jeep trail across the tundra.

Old Carson, with its big, old, swaybacked buildings constructed of huge logs, hauled up from timberline far below.

14.

EUREKA

THE TOWN of Eureka is nestled deep in the mountains of San Juan County and takes its name from Eureka Gulch, just west of the townsite. During the 1860's, gold seekers, believing they had struck it rich here, gave the name Eureka, a Greek word meaning "I have found it," to the entire region. Ferdinand Vandeveer Hayden of the United States Geological Survey, who visited the camp several years later, said, "We came out into a big clump of trees among which were several big cabins, bearing on a signboard the name "Eureka," evidently intended for the name of a town that was expected to be. Though what had been found there to suggest the name was not immediately apparent."

The small mining camp that grew up around this point was founded in the 1870's. Crofutt described it as being situated in the extreme northern part of Baker's Park, named for Charles Baker, the old mountain man of Colorado's fur-trade period. In the 1870's it was described as being situated on Post Road No. 30, north from Silverton nine miles and five miles south from Animas Forks, fare fifteen cents per mile by stagecoach. At first the town consisted of a store, one hotel, a dozen buildings and one smelting works. The *San Juan Expositor* was the name of a monthly newspaper that was published there. The principal ore-producing mines were the McKinney, the Boomerang, and the Yellow Jacket. The ores of this region in general were galena of a high type, accompanied by the presence of gray copper. Some of the best property at this point was locked up in litigation, which was regarded as a certain guarantee that it was rich in minerals.

Chief sources of Eureka's wealth were the old Sunnyside Mine and mill, once the largest in the state. It was located in 1873 and was almost a constant producer until it closed temporarily in 1931.

The history of Eureka was constantly punctuated by accounts of the disastrous rock slides that roared down upon the residents from the extremely steep, treeless slopes that flank the town on two sides. Unlike many of these early towns, Eureka was not deserted in the last century.

The *Silverton Standard* for August 2, 1937, carried the following account:

Eureka is the center of activity for the past few weeks. Over 50 men are busy preparing the various equipment for operation of the famous Sunnyside mine. A steam shovel is building a dam at the mill's tailings pond below Eureka. The Sunnyside mill is being thoroughly reconditioned. The crew is cleaning out the portal of the mine and the mine boardinghouse has been opened to accommodate this crew. Several families have moved to Eureka from Silverton and several more houses have been allotted to employees for occupancy in the near future.

On August 16 of that same year, this report was carried by the *Grand Junction Daily Sentinel:*

The town of Eureka met recently and organized to tend to the affairs of San Juan County's second largest city in size. Since the Sunnyside closed down about seven years ago, little attention has been paid to Eureka town government. Since that city has been growing rapidly, the need of city organization was felt.

The decline began in 1939 when the *Silverton Standard* reported the following on December 22:

The Eureka, San Juan County, Colorado Post Office will be discontinued on 12/30/39. All mail for that post office will be received, delivered, and accounted for by the post office at Silverton.

But this was not the end. The following report appeared on October 12, 1940:

> The Sunnyside mill at Eureka was started up Monday and is steadily running day and night. The machinery runs smooth as glass and the concentrators are doing splendid work. A great many hundred tons of ore are stored in the bins and there is a big reserve still to break from the same mine.

At last the mill closed during World War II and was never reopened. The final curtain was run down in 1948 when the huge Sunnyside was sold for $225,000 and dismantled for salvage.

The town of Eureka is reasonably accessible over quite an acceptable auto road and is situated nine miles north of Silverton on State Highway 110.

If you have a Jeep and are coming from almost any other direction, it is shorter and quicker to follow the instructions given for reaching Animas Forks, after crossing either Cinnamon or Engineer Pass. From Animas Forks, at the foot of either pass, turn left (south) and drive the old abandoned bed of Otto Mears's Silverton-Northern Railroad down into Eureka. Today this trail is barely more than a passable groove in the mountainside that takes you down the Animas River Canyon. As you emerge on the last ledge, you will enjoy looking down upon an exquisite, broad, green valley, deeply scarred by attempts at civilization. Several hundred feet below you the silvery stream of the Animas winds across the valley floor. This is the site of what remains at Eureka. The few tottering structures and the large gaping foundations mark the site of the town's main street. The huge diagonal scar, beginning at the foot of the trail, was the site of the Sunnyside mill stretching up the terraced mountainside across from the town on your right.

One building, situated in the center of Eureka, has aroused much curiosity. It is a high, oblong building, much like a tower without windows. Some people in Silverton thought it was the jail; others believed it had been the town's fire-house; still others have expressed the idea that it was the pay office for the mines. The most recent speculation has it rumored as a place where fire hoses were hung up to dry. It is still standing.

At the north end of the valley, several log cabins remain but the old false-fronted structures of later vintage that once lined Eureka's main street fell down three winters ago.

Today, Eureka is a completely dead town in every sense of the word. By 1980 the cabins at the northeast end of the meadow had disintegrated markly. Soon all traces of this settlement will be erased.

---

* In this same area see also Animas Forks, Gladstone, Howardsville, Middleton, and Mineral Point.

Courtesy Library, State Historical Society of Colorado
This is a very early photograph of Eureka

Cabins at the north end of Eureka townsite in 1948

Looking south down the principal street of Eureka

15.

FLORESTA

NOT EVERY ghost camp in Colorado had its origin in the gold- or silver-mining industries. Marble grew up and prospered around stone quarrying. Black Hawk, with few mines to produce its wealth, gained prominence as a great refining center, while Como was best known for its roundhouse and the role it played in early railroad transportation in South Park. Floresta, located deep in the mountain and forest fastness of Gunnison County, is still another example of a present-day ghost town that flourished during the mining period and yet produced no silver or gold. The economic reason for the town's existence was a tremendous body of fine-grade anthracite coal. The main deposit extended from Crested Butte through Irwin to Floresta and as far west as Somerset. The mine at this point was called the Floresta and was owned and operated by the Colorado Fuel and Iron Company. The town that grew up before the turn of the present century was first known as Ruby-Anthracite. A good wagon road made it something of a local shipping center for the region, and a stagecoach from Gunnison served its transportation needs. The closest bank was at Crested Butte. As prosperity and the market for good coal increased, a railroad was pushed through from Crested Butte and the former name was dropped. Since that time it has been called Floresta.

The chronology of the camp is unclear. One source dates it from "before the turn of the century" to 1936. A second reference places its life span between the years 1902 and

1919. Its railroad was abandond in 1929. At any rate, the population usually fluctuated between 100 and 250 people who operated the camp until winter made it uninhabitable, usually until January. The winter snows packed into the basin that holds the town to a depth of twenty-five feet, and a trip out in any direction meant climbing "up over."

The company worked on back orders throughout much of its history. Due to winter lumbering operations, a large number of trees can still be seen that were topped in winter at or above the twenty-five-foot mark.

Lack of adequate all-weather transportation and the declining coal market spelled doom for Floresta. Today, its straight line of roofless cabins, nestled in a deep, lush, green meadow, is fast being overgrown. A large stone building, still fairly intact, stands at the upper end of the town.

The best route in begins by driving north from Crested Butte, keeping left at the only fork in the road, until you reach the point where several roads intersect from Irwin and Kebler Pass. Take the road that goes left past the sawmill until you reach a battered Forest Service marker which says, "Floresta 3." Follow the sign, keeping left at the next intersection to the logging camp. Here it would be well to make inquiries since the road is more than a little "mushy" in spots until at least mid-July, and when last seen some tremendous trees had fallen across the trail about a half mile short of the town, necessitating a short walk.

The route described was the wagon road. The railroad grade, which was much shorter, has fallen away badly and cannot be driven by Jeep. A more thrilling route than the road in from Crested Butte, up to the top of Kebler Pass, is to take the road from Gunnison north toward the butte for approximately five miles. Here you turn left, taking the old road through the ghost towns of Baldwin, Mount Carbon, and on toward Ohio Pass. Before making the ascent of the pass, one may observe, off to the east, the great unfinished rock palisades of the Irwin branch of the Denver,

South Park and Pacific Railway. Irwin never got its railroad due to the mines playing out in 1882. From this point, an additional mile and a half will bring you to the turnoff for Floresta. The wagon road may prove to be passable for all but the newest cars with little clearance underneath, depending upon its condition at any given time. Local inquiries are advisable. Anyway, it's an extremely long three miles.*

*In this same area see also Gothic, Ruby-Irwin, and Tin Cup.

Summer homes, cabins, and shaft hoist at Gilpin, named for Colorado's first territorial governor.

Roofless foundations at Floresta, a coal camp

16.

GILPIN

In 1861 President Abraham Lincoln signed the appointment making his close personal friend, William Gilpin, the first governor of the newly created territory of Colorado. No stranger to the West, Gilpin had previously accompanied John C. Fremont to Oregon in 1843, had served as a major in the War with Mexico, and had led a campaign against the Plains Indians in 1848. Widely known as a lecturer, he had also written a book describing the resources of the West and predicting a great future for the region. Because of this he was sometimes called the "John the Baptist of the West."

Since statehood was not granted until 1876, selection of territorial officials was not yet accomplished by popular vote. Instead, such officials are still appointed by the President of the United States. Too often the official appointed knew little and cared less for the region he was sent to govern since he often received the job as a political plum under the spoils system.

In view of Gilpin's interests and wealth of previous experience, Lincoln's appointment by comparison, was like a light in the wilderness. The news was particularly well received in Colorado, though Gilpin's arrival did not materialize for an additional two months.

Shortly after he assumed his duties at Denver, a small mining camp grew up near Gamble Gulch and was named Gilpin in honor of the new governor. In addition to a small mine within the immediate environs of the camp, the War

Eagle and Gettysburg mines were developed nearby and contributed to the economic basis of the town. Additional discoveries on Lump Gulch failed to pan out as expected and the growth of Gilpin was curtailed. It was never a large settlement and its place in the sun diminished with the ascension of its richer contemporary, Perigo, which was located nearby.

Two roads, both with good dirt surfaces, serve Gilpin today. The first leaves the paved highway, State 119, about a mile south of Rollinsville and follows the contours of Gamble Gulch for three miles, at which point you turn left and drive two more miles to Gilpin. The second road leaves the same paved highway about four miles south of Rollinsville and follows Lump Gulch for two miles to the

By 1980 Gilpin had become a development of summer homes. Two original structures still stand, the rest is only a memory.

---

* In this same area see also Baltimore and Caribou.

17.

GLADSTONE

THE EARLIEST mining activity in this neighborhood was at Poughkeepsie, near the head of the gulch by the same name. In 1879 a road was built up Cement Creek from Silverton to connect it with the Poughkeepsie district. That same year, some chlorination works had been put in on this road at a point nine miles northeast of Silverton. This was the beginning of Gladstone, named for the prime minister of Great Britain. The Sampson Mine was discovered nearby in 1882 and worked actively throughout the later eighties. Then, in 1887, an employee of the Sampson, Olaf Nelson, discovered the Gold King vein nearby and worked it on a limited scale until his death in 1890. Four years later his widow sold the property for $15,000. Later that same year a concentrator was installed, shafts were expanded, and many nearby claims were acquired and incorporated into the Gold King holdings. It became the area's largest producer and was, in fact, the mine that made Gladstone.

With expanding prosperity, a population of two hundred, and glowing prospects for the future, the inevitable narrow-gauge railroad was constructed up the creek in 1899 to serve the trade and traffic needs of this growing community. As with Eureka and Red Mountain Town, the railway builder was Otto Mears, who named this line the Silverton, Gladstone, and Northerly. It continued in operation for the first decade and a half of the present century; the tracks were dismantled and removed in 1926.

A fire in 1907 destroyed much of the Gold King real

estate above the tunnel and several men lost their lives as
a result of smoke inhalation. A further setback came about
in 1910 when lawsuits among the owners and stockholders
developed and forced a shutdown of the property. Some
mining has been done off and on since that time. At present
the town is filled with heavy construction equipment and
huge pipes for use in the proposed American Tunnel which
is to be built in order to connect a number of old mining
properties scattered here and there among the surrounding
mountains.

From Silverton, the road up Cement Creek is passable for
any vehicle all the way to Gladstone. The concrete stair-steps
stretching up the mountainside are all that remain of the
foundation of the Grand Mogul mill. The several weather-
beaten buildings at the south edge of the town were a
part of the original community and are identifiable from
old photographs in the Western History Collection of the
Denver Public Library. There are a number of new roads,
also identifiable by comparison with old photographs which
show the old, now partly overgrown thoroughfares of the
original town. Gone are the long rows of small, identical,
white, company-owned houses that once characterized and
identified Gladstone. Beyond the town, the trail continues
on to Ouray. Statements as to its present condition, however, are conflicting and its passability remains an unresolved
question mark.*

By 1980 all of the buildings shown in the accompanying
photographs were gone.

---

* In this same area see also Animas Forks, Eureka, Howardsville, Middleton, and Red Mountain Town.

Culvert pipes and a few of the cabins at Gladstone, up Cement Creek from Silverton

The stair-step ruins of the Grand Mogul mill and the swaybacked cabins at Gladstone

18.

GOLD HILL

THE HAND OF posterity has laid a heavy and compulsive hold on the history of Gold Hill in terms of an impressive list of "firsts." For here, so 't is said, there was discovered on January 15, 1859, the very first lode gold in what was to become Colorado Territory. Some historians say that the placer deposits discovered earlier on Gold Run, below the present town, constituted the first discovery of gold of any variety in the region, while others credit the discovery to George A. Jackson, of Missouri. The chronology is confused. The Jackson discovery was made early in January near where Chicago Creek empties into Clear Creek but was kept a secret until May when $1,900 was taken out in a single week. The time schedule is further confused by the January prospecting of John H. Gregory on the north fork of Clear Creek. Returning in May, he struck the fabled Gregory Lode at Mountain City, which produced $472 in four days.

This would seem to leave clear title to the claim of Gold Hill to the first discovery of lode gold and perhaps to the placer variety as well. At any rate, Gold Hill did become the first permanent mining camp in Colorado. Historians further agree that the first mining district was organized here on March 7, 1859, but differ as to its name. Since the area was then a part of Nebraska, one source lists it as Mountain District No. 1 of Nebraska, while another calls it the Gold Hill Mining District. The Gregory District was not organized until two months later.

That autumn saw the erection of a quartz stamp mill at the base of the hill which also qualified as the first such piece of machinery in operation within the region. It had been freighted across the plains by ox teams, as was virtually every other commodity which reached Colorado at this period in history. The first producing vein was the Scott, followed by the Horsfal, Alamakee, and Cold Spring. A number of placers were also worked actively, and several of the picturesque arrastras were used in the stream beds to refine their output.

The town itself was built at an elevation of 8,500 feet and housed about 1,500 people. When the surface ores played out in 1861, there was a temporary exodus until the Hill smelter at Black Hawk began its profitable treatment of the more refractory ores. The year 1872 saw a second rush to Gold Hill after tellurium ores were discovered there. Due to the highly transitory nature of most early prospectors, any attempts to arrive at accurate census statistics were difficult. The population figure of one thousand seems to be accepted as about right during this second boom.

A number of hotels, newspapers, and the customary commercial enterprises flourished here. One of the best known was erected in 1872 and was called the Mines Hotel. Frequent references have been made to the fact that Eugene Field, during his brief sojourn as a Denver newspaper reporter, immortalized this establishment in one of his poems. It is still standing but has had its exterior face-lifted somewhat. Currently, it is owned and operated by the Chicago Holiday Association and secretaries from the big city relax here in the summer. The miners, in an early local-option election, unanimously rejected saloons, depending instead upon community dances, singing clubs, and literary societies for their after-hours diversions.

The road to Gold Hill is a particularly well-marked one. Take State Highway 119 west out of Boulder to the marked intersection on your right which says "Salina, Gold Hill" and then follow the signs. Actually, there are several other good roads, all dirt, and most of them are shown on any good highway map of the state.

Unlike many of its nearby contemporaries, Gold Hill has never given up the ghost, despite two disastrous fires that swept the town. A small permanent population still resides here, supplemented by the summer influx. Its location, nearly on the hilltop, with the great snow-crested peaks to the northwest, make it a particularly attractive community.*

Since this chapter was written, the hip-roofed Walter house has burned; but the rest of the town is as described.

---

* In this same area see also Magnolia and Wall Street.

Gold Hill, still going strong! The Arapahoe peaks are behind the town

19.

GOLD PARK

THE TOWN OF Gold Park was located on Homestake Creek, a stream which separates the French Mountain spur from the Homestake. On both of these spurs, evidence of lime was found, which encouraged the prospectors to look for carbonates. This seemed especially promising since the area was in a direct line between Leadville and the newer carbonate discoveries in Garfield County. Founding of the town occurred in 1880, and life was quiet until the following year. This account appeared in the *Leadville Herald Democrat,* 1922:

December 4, 1881 was a day of great excitement in the town of Gold Park in what is now Eagle County. H. Weston, foreman of the G. P. Mining Co. was shot and killed by a man named Bagley, a discharged blacksmith. Bagley also made an unsuccessful attempt to shoot superintendent Turney. He then fortified himself in his cabin which was immediately surrounded by a mob. The cabin was beseiged for eight hours without success. Finally, a large quantity of giant powder was placed near the door and the case ignited. The explosion which followed tore the cabin to pieces and Bagley was found with a bullet hole through his heart, evidently having committed suicide. Bagley had friends who then threatened Turney's life and an armed guard was placed around his cabin day and night. Jay White and other friends of Bagley, who were ordered out of town by the vigilantes, paraded the streets of town all one day looking for the committee but left town at night.

Perhaps this next account, which was printed in the April 18, 1883, issue of the *Rocky Mountain News,* was an attempt to live down the previous account:

The morals of the place are above the average for mining camps since the output of the mines has never been large enough to attract the various elements that usually invade thrifty camps. The needed thing most sadly felt by all citizens is a post route as all mail service as yet has been carried by persons paid out of a fund subscribed here.

At this time there were two stores in nearby Holy Cross City but only one in Gold Park. A school and church were put up in the summer of 1883. That same year, in April, the *Rocky Mountain News* reported that a branch line of the Denver and Rio Grande Railway was surveyed to Gold Park but did not get beyond the planning stage. A large, successful, and satisfactory reduction works was located at Gold Park and was operated by the Gold Park Mining Company, a corporation which also controlled most other aspects of the town's life. The reduction works not only processed local ores, but also those carried down through a direct two-mile-long flume from Holy Cross City. This latter town was also owned and controlled by the Gold Park Mining Company.

The road to Gold Park is a completely safe one for even the newer cars. On U.S. Highway 24 north of Leadville, turn left (west) just beyond Pando and before reaching Redcliff and keep on the dirt road that follows Homestake Creek for the nine miles to Gold Park. Only two log cabins remain to mark the site of this community that once exceeded nearby Holy Cross City in size. These cabins, close together, are to be found in a meadow at the left side of the road. From this point, the road narrows into a trail as it leaves the sheltered clearing that contains the remains of Gold Park. If in doubt about the location, there is a red Forest Service emergency box at the right side of the road at this point. Travel beyond this meadow in anything other than a Jeep is unwise.

Today, the area is sometimes used as a campsite and occasionally as a starting point for hikers or fishermen who wish to explore the surrounding wilderness.*

---

* In this same area see also Holy Cross City, Vicksburg, and Winfield.

Gold Park. Both cabins now gone.

Dr. Gerald G. Coon, my son Marshall, and "Count" crossing one of the bridges in a typical section of the unholy road to Holy Cross City.

20.

GOTHIC

IN SEPTEMBER of 1878 Truman Blancett rode his horse and led a pack mule loaded with supplies over the range, descending into the valley where Gothic now stands. Making his camp under a tree, he prospected six hundred dollars in wire silver out of the area before the first snow fell. This act earned him the distinction of being the first man to mine this region. He stated later that he told only two people about his discovery; but when he returned in the spring of 1879 to resume mining, two hundred persons were there.

When he was well past eighty years of age, Blancett returned to Gothic in 1928 for a visit. He located the stump of the tree under which he originally camped and discussed the early history of Gothic with students of the Rocky Mountain Biological Laboratory. Sometimes referred to as "the Last of the Old Scouts," Blancett lived to be one hundred and two or one hundred and three and passed away in New York in 1942.

Gothic was the most important mining camp in Gunnison County during the 1880's. It was established first as a boom town in June of 1879, and the census of the next year gave it a population of 950 souls. Earlier that same year James Jennings discovered the Sylvanite Mine, which had not been equaled for richness of silver ore up to that time. In driving tunnels they came at intervals to pockets of native wire silver. These specimens were passed around, and by the spring of the next year there was another great rush of people to Gothic.

The town itself was founded by Sam Weil, and it took on a rapid growth beginning in 1880 when cabins sprang up all over the tiny valley at the foot of Gothic Mountain. Gothic became the supply depot or outfitting point for many small mining camps in the vicinity and for the hundreds of prospectors who were packing into the mountains in every direction. There was quite a bit of traffic between Gunnison on the one side of Schofield Pass and Carbondale and Glenwood Springs on the other. When Crofutt, the well-known author of the *Grip-Sack Guide,* visited the camp, he recorded the following interesting observation. "There are none here for their health, yet it is a healthy country, a poor place for physicians."

The *Elk Mountain Bonanza,* a weekly, was the area's first newspaper. In the spring of 1880 Willis Sweet brought another paper to Gothic and named it the *Miner.* Sweet was financed by Horace A. W. Tabor, but one year was enough and Sweet departed for Idaho. On June 30 of 1882 Gothic acquired a third paper, called the *Silver Record.*

Large supplies of food were brought in and stores and gambling kept pace with the boom. Hotels, boardinghouses, shops, saloons, one smelter, three sawmills, a public school, dance hall—everything was there, including a preacher. The chief hotels were the Olds and the Burns. The Olds Hotel was built in 1880. However, it soon changed its name to the Grant Hotel because former President Ulysses S. Grant stayed there upon returning from his round-the-world trip that same year. Later photographs seem to indicate that this second name was dropped in favor of the more appropriate "Gothic Hotel."

Uncle Charlie and Mother Howe also kept a small hotel in Gothic. They were typical New Englanders from Vermont, and their place was a haven of rest to many a weary traveler.

Four to five thousand people soon made their homes in Gothic, all of them busy in commerce, freighting, or mining. The Sylvanite Mine was located at the head of Copper Creek, some four miles from Gothic and near the road that goes over the divide and down Maroon Creek to Aspen. The Sylvanite Company was always tinkering with the mill. They never seemed to get the kind of equipment that would save the values in their ore. They would start on a mill in the spring and get it ready for treating the minerals late in the fall. Next they would put a run through and then shut down for the winter. Next spring they were ready to take out the equipment and try something else that some machinery house had advised them to buy. This process was kept up repeatedly until everyone grew old and the price of silver went so low that interest was lost in trying to do anything with the mine.

To reach Gothic at the present time, drive north from Crested Butte through the East River Valley on State Highway 327 for a distance of nine miles. The buildings remaining at the site are situated on the east bank of the East River at the junction with Copper Creek. On the opposite side, across from the town, Gothic Mountain rises to an altitude of 12,570 feet. Another, but more difficult, approach to Gothic may be made by crossing old Schofield Pass from the Crystal River Valley. This carries you over some grand and beautiful scenery but the route is suitable only for Jeeps or hikers.

The story of Gothic is, in many ways, the story of Garwood H. Judd, sometimes called the man who stayed, or the last mayor of Gothic. When the rush came to Leadville in the early seventies and eighties, the overflow reached Gothic where, in 1878, high-grade lead and silver ores had been discovered. In the next four years claims on Elk Mountain, Copper Creek, and the East River were heavy producers. Judd came to Gothic in the 1880's and stayed for the rest of his life.

When silver slumped, the thousands of gold and silver seekers left for richer fields; but Garwood Judd stayed on.

He died May 15, 1930, in Crested Butte, at the age of seventy-eight. Complying with his last wish, his friends saw that his body was cremated, and the next summer when the heart of the Elk Mountains was fired with the color of columbines, the ashes of Judd were scattered over Gothic. Because of this, many people say that he's still there.

Today the population of Gothic has been replaced with a new breed of prospectors. Scientists and students have been meeting here every summer for thirty-five years to hunt the secrets of mountain wildlife. The scattered buildings are now the home of the Rocky Mountain Biological Laboratory, founded by Dr. John C. Johnston. Animals, birds, and flowers are found in rich variety on Gothic's doorstep. The front yard is a biologist's vertical slice of the high Rockies. With the coming of the laboratory, Gothic has acquired a new lease on life.*

---

* In the same area see also Floresta, Ruby-Irwin, and Tin Cup.

Collection of Dr. John C. Johnston

An early photograph showing the town of Gothic as it appeared in 1880

The city hall at Gothic

Some of the cabins at Gothic, and the road leading to Schofield Pass

21.

HANCOCK

HANCOCK had the reputation of being a thrifty town. It was founded in 1880 as a station on the Denver, South Park, and Pacific Railway, and was located two miles below the eastern end of the great Alpine Tunnel. A limited amount of prospecting was done here, mostly for galena, but this was one community where mining took a back seat to the railroad and specifically to the Alpine Tunnel, which Hancock was built to serve. The tunnel itself was 1,805 feet long, 14 feet wide, and 17 feet in height.

The townsite was laid out twenty-two miles west of Nathrop and ten miles from Alpine in a sheltered valley at the headwaters of Chalk Creek, with high snow-capped peaks on all sides. In 1881 the town consisted of five stores, a hotel, some restaurants, several saloons, two sawmills, and a resident population of several hundred in addition to the transient railroad workers. Mark Twain, the noted American humorist and writer, was one among the several notable persons who visited Hancock in its heyday. Upon his arrival in the town he described the two-mile-long ride down from the Alpine Tunnel as one of the most hair-raising experiences of his life.

The last sale of a lot was recorded in 1885, which nearly marked the town's end as a place of importance. Many residents, however, continued to live at Hancock until the turn of the present century.

To see Hancock now, follow the directions given for getting to St. Elmo and Romley. From Romley, continue climb-

ing up along the same road for another mile to the ruins
of the huge Flora Belle Mine on your left. The unusual
blue-gray of the road is due to cinders and the fact that this
was once the railroad bed. The old ties and rails were torn
out and salvaged many years ago and modern county grading
equipment had transformed the old right-of-way into quite
a good road.

Beyond the mine, where the road enters an open meadow
and crosses a small bridge, was the site of Hancock. The
building on your left was a bar and is all that remains of
a long row of buildings that once lined the main street.
Across the meadow, where the trees have sheltered them,
are a few additional cabins. All the rest of this once-proud
community is gone.

From this area two roads leave the town. The first goes
to the right and follows the abandoned grade of the Denver,
South Park, and Pacific Railway to the Alpine Tunnel.
About two hundred yards beyond Hancock on this same
road, still another trail goes up very sharply to the left and
crosses old Williams Pass by way of the historic and beautiful
Palisade of the Denver, South Park, and Pacific Railway.
Due to a huge bog at the top of the pass, this should be
attempted only in dry weather, and even then it is a road
to try the endurance and patience of the hardiest Jeep drivers.
The road brings you out across from State Highway 162.
Drive through the bed of Quartz Creek and up the opposite
bank to reach the road. The other road leaving Hancock
goes to Alpine or Hancock Pass, and, though easier than
Williams, is still a Jeep road. It comes out eventually on
State Highway 162 near Pitkin.*

By 1980 the old saloon was sagging badly. A few other
remains of cabins can still be found.

---

* In this same area see also Quartz, Romley, St. Elmo, Tin Cup, and Woodstock.

The town saloon (at left) and the few cabins still standing at Hancock, near the headwaters of Chalk Creek.

One cabin and the well-known three domed peak, long a landmark at Hancock

Believe it or not, a typical stretch of the old wagon road across Williams Pass

22.

HOLY CROSS CITY

HOLY CROSS CITY is a silent and empty place today. The old wagon trail to the town is one of the most remarkable roads in the state. For over three quarters of a century this alpine ghost camp has been quiet. The small number of original cabins have escaped being stripped by the claws of scavengers only because of the nastiness of the trail up from Gold Park. Holy Cross City is situated at the eastern foot of French Mountain. By wagon road it is about thirty-seven miles northwest of Leadville, though only about twenty miles away in a direct line. Homestake Mountain lies between these two points and deflects travel to the above extent.

There is only one acceptable route to Holy Cross City today. It is approached by State Highway 24 north from Leadville to Pando. About three miles beyond Pando you turn off west or left down a winding dirt road that follows Homestake Creek to the two cabins that mark the remains of the once thriving camp of Gold Park. Holy Cross City and Gold Park both lie within a radius of five miles and both had claims that were promising enough for treatment or shipment. About thirty claims in the region were owned by the Gold Park Mining Company.

At Gold Park you have a choice of two routes. The steepest, narrowest, and rockiest is the trail to Holy Cross City and goes up to your right. The other goes straight ahead and leads to some desirable fishing water. The distance up from Gold Park to Holy Cross City is only four bone-shaking miles but you should plan on spending about one and a half nerve-wracking hours behind the wheel of your Jeep to get there over one of the steepest, roughest and toughest of mountain roads. The rough, rocky contours of the trail wind upward in corkscrew curves with only the road itself between imposing precipices above and yawning chasms below.

You will drive across paths of old logs that the pioneers called a corduroy road, over broken-down bridges that leave no room for guesswork, through bogs and streams and over huge boulders and sharp, high rocks, strategically emerging from the trail and so placed as to twist the frame of the Jeep in two opposite directions at once. At such times one may hear the comforting sound of the fan blades scraping on the housing. There are two forks along the trail—keep right at the first and left at the second. Both lead back to the original trail but the first contains impassable boulders and the second has a swamp, invisible under the tall grass until you're in it up to the axles. All this while you're still climbing sharply upwards.

Finally, you'll switch around a deep curve and enter a section heavily fringed with dense pines and you're almost there. Now, around the shattered remains of the Holy Cross mill, long ago burned, that used to be connected by a two-and-a-half-mile-long direct flume to Gold Park, almost directly below. Holy Cross City is barely beyond the mill in a sheltered, nearly timberline meadow to your right. The altitude at this point is 11,335 feet above sea level. Back of the town are great dome-shaped hills covered with evergreens, and beyond tower the lofty peaks. These mountains are an unceasing wonder; none of them is snow-clad in August, yet they tower high enough toward the sky to veil their heads in the clouds. Here the busy workaday world is shut out and a quiet, peaceful quality pervades this great cathedral of nature.

Due to the prevalence of swamps and bogs around Holy

Cross City, it is safer to leave your vehicle and walk the fifty or so yards into the town where a few cabins and about seventeen foundations remain. Despite one write-up to the contrary, the famed Mount of the Holy Cross, source of the town's name, is not visible from the town itself and a topographical map reveals that an additional range of mountains in between prevents one from being able to see it from this point.

The trail continues on beyond the town and is far more hazardous and better suited to walking. If followed, it eventually brings you out atop Fancy Pass about two miles beyond.

In the early eighties Holy Cross City was a roaring, vigorous town whose mines were rich enough to support the establishment of a school district. The peak population, before the inevitable decline, approached three hundred people. One hotel, the Timberline, was built and prospered during the life of the camp. The town also supported an assay office and a justice of the peace.

The Gold Park Mining Company made many improvements on their large number of claims at or near the townsite. In addition, a Pennsylvania syndicate owned a rich mine known by the eternally popular name of the Comstock, which was believed to have been an extension of the famous Grand Trunk, the best developed lode on that side of French Mountain. Other great mines were the Hunky Dory and the Belle of the West.

The mail was brought in several times each week from Redcliff by stagecoach. Dr. H. W. Roby, the resident manager of the Gold Park Mining Company, also acted as the postmaster.

Despite all this, the life of the camp was a comparatively short one. After only a few years the company began to realize that the mines simply could not produce sufficient ore to keep the books out of the red and the bills paid. Late in 1883 some of the miners began the long trek back down the hill. The ore deposits that had once been regarded as promising were very short-lived now and by the 1890's even Dr. Roby and his wife, who had stayed on long after the others had gone, left the town.

Today the big boilers of the huge Holy Cross mill are exposed and rusting among blackened timbers at the mill-site, while all but a few of the cabins have fallen before the relentless onslaught of nature's severest elements, alone and all but forgotten in the hectic rush of the twentieth century.*

---

* In this same area see also Gold Park, Vicksburg, and Winfield.

Ruined cabins and the swampy meadow at old Holy Cross City, above Homestake Creek

*Looking back over the cabins and foundations of Holy Cross City
from the Fancy Pass road.*

23.

HOWARDSVILLE

THE TOWN OF Howardsville, although it lost its post office, still has a small permanent population. All mail today comes through Silverton, where most of the town's population is employed. It is reached by following State Highway 110 north of Silverton. The town is situated on the Animas River at the mouth of Cunningham Gulch, five miles above Silverton and four miles south of Eureka.

Except for the contour of the hillside across from the town, there is little resemblance to old photographs of Howardsville as most of the original buildings are gone and nearly all of the present structures are those of the twentieth century.

The entire San Juan country was known as Baker's Park back in 1861 when it was first explored by Charles Baker, pioneer mountain man of Colorado's fur-trade period. He was the first white man to enter the area which, at that time, was still Ute Indian territory. His camp is said to have been where Silverton now stands, but he prospected through the Animas Valley as far as Eureka.

Howardsville was founded in 1874 and served as the first seat of newly formed San Juan County, after the Brunot Treaty with the Utes opened the area to prospecting and settlement. At that time Stony Pass, up Cunningham Gulch, was the only practical means of access over the high and forbidding San Juans.

The village proper consisted of several stores, the in-evitable saloons, one small reduction works, approximately thirty buildings of all kinds, and a population of 150 hardy persons.

Up Cunningham Gulch, above and to the east of Howardsville, were a number of very rich paying properties. In addition to the valuable Niegold concentration works, once called Niegoldstown, there were the Pride of the West, Philadelphia, Green Mountain, Shenandoah, Bruce, and the notable Highland Mary mines.

Howardsville has had its ups and downs along with the fluctuations of mining fortunes. At the present time it is more than holding its own in the twentieth-century battle for survival.*

Some new mining was begun in the area in the 1970's.

---

* In this same area see also Animas Forks, Eureka, Gladstone, Middleton, and Mineral Point.

*Howardsville, in the Animas Valley northeast of Silverton.
This view was taken looking west.*

*The long, straight, main street of Ironton, south of Ouray,
looking back toward Red Mountain Pass.*

24.

IRONTON

THE EXCITEMENT of the Red Mountain district overflowed down the north side of the pass in 1882 and resulted in the founding of Ironton. It grew up and prospered as a residence center for the miners who worked in the depths of the nearby Yankee Girl and Guston mines, which produced both silver and lead.

Further prosperity arrived in 1889 when Otto Mears extended his narrow-gauge Rainbow Route on down the mountain where it terminated in Ironton Park. Plans to extend the line the remaining distance to Ouray were buried under insurmountable odds and the remaining tracks were never laid. The long, broad, and level valley in which the town was built made it a natural center of transportation and supply activities where coaches from Ouray could meet the railroad and where burro pack trains could be outfitted to service the surrounding mines.

The history of Carson was repeated once again at Ironton in 1898. With the fall of silver support prices, the fortunes of the town began to wane until gold was found nearby. This started another rush and the development of new shafts running far deeper into the mountainside. As drilling continued, the nature of the ores changed to reveal the presence of copper. The underground water, almost always present in deep mines, contributed an additional hazard when it was found to contain deadly sulphuric acid which corroded the tools and equipment. The Joker tunnel, an underground bore from the Yankee Girl, was completed in 1906 and was successful in alleviating the hazard.

Although some mining operations still continue in the area, the men no longer reside on the single long main street that was Ironton. As you drop down from the top of Red Mountain Pass on U.S. 550, the road straightens out below the switchbacks and levels off where it traverses Ironton Park. The townsite was off to the east about fifty yards and ran parallel with the present highway. Until a few years ago, many of the original structures remained, but now only a few houses at the south end, and long rows of empty foundations, mark the site.*

* In this same area see also Mineral Point, Red Mountain Town, and Sneffels.

25.

LAMARTINE

LAMARTINE, located high in the mountains behind Idaho Springs, is the town that many people have tried and failed to reach due to a multiplicity of roads that literally honeycomb the hillsides above west Chicago Creek. The easiest way to Lamartine involves following Trail Creek from the point where it leaves U.S. Highway 40 west of Idaho Springs. Drive through Freeland, keeping to your right where the road forks. From this point the trail becomes steeper, climbing up through a large abandoned mine and finally coming out on top after several switchbacks. The huge old Lamartine Mine will be on your right, laid out against a backdrop of spectacular Front Range peaks.

A second route, more complicated, steeper, and much more difficult, goes up Ute Creek Canyon from State Highway 103, five miles southwest of the bridge at Idaho Springs. The road climbs steeply up past the original site of the Idaho Springs waterwheel. A well-preserved stamp mill with shaker tables, cams, and several big stamps still in place will be seen on your right a mile or so beyond the wheel site. Beyond the stamp mill, take the third turn to your right and an even steeper and rockier trail eventually will lead you into the high alpine meadow containing Lamartine's few remaining cabins, nestled in the edge of the trees.

Lamartine was a one-mine town and the population was never more than five hundred. Development of the mine started in 1887 and production of gold, silver, and lead continued sporadically until about the turn of the present century. The town is laid out on quite a steep hillside with the mine at the crest and the houses ranging like stairsteps down the hill with one rooftop in line with the next cabin's foundation. The active life of Lamartine covered only about two decades, with the end coming early in the twentieth century.

Mostly roofless log walls marked Lamartine's site in 1980.

One of the few remaining structures at Lamartine,
high in the mountains above Idaho Springs.

Scattered foundations, a cabin, and cows at the site of Lamartine

26.

THE LONDON MINES

THE NORTH and South London Mines are included here as being representatives of a less common type of mining community that flourished in Colorado during the 1880's. They were located in 1883 and due more to the influence of geography than to any other factors, small settlements grew up around the mines. Situated rather remotely away from the established population centers of the Mosquito district, it would have been difficult and probably impossible for the miners to commute to their work. These communities were small and somewhat on the order of early twentieth-century company towns, except that they were never incorporated formally. The North London mill and its cabins may still be seen by following the north fork of Mosquito Gulch for the seven miles west from Alma. The remaining structures are on the north slope of London Mountain. State Highway 9, north from Fairplay, will carry you toward Alma. At the south edge of the latter town, turn left on State Highway 300. This is the road to Mosquito Pass. Up the gulch a few miles the road forks. Take the right turn to the cabins, the remains of the North London boarding-houses and bunkhouses.

The South London Mine is situated nearby on the eastern slope of Mosquito Pass. Again, follow State Highway 9 north from Fairplay to Alma. Leave the highway just south of town where the Mosquito Pass sign directs you to a dirt road branching off to the left. At the fork of the

road, go left until you arrive at the South London Mine
and its collection of cabins where the workers lived.

Historically, the claims were 300 x 1,500 feet each and
were owned by the London Mines Incorporated, chartered
under the laws of the state of New York in New York City
and at Fairplay, Colorado. Developments at the North London included two tunnels on the vein, one hundred and
five hundred feet long respectively. One of these was called
the London and the second was called the Hard to Beat. A
large amount of stoping was done which showed huge quantities of ore reserves and over a half mile of ore veins. Steam-
powered machinery was used and a 4,500-foot-long wire
tramway connected the mine up on top with the London,
South Park and Leadville Railway, a six-mile length of
track built especially for the transportation of ore from
the mine to the company's mill at London Junction. This
mill was a large one containing twenty stamps for crushing the ore. The output from the mines was one hundred
tons per day. Seventy-five hundred feet of ventilating pipe
supplied the lower levels of the mine with fresh air.

The top layer of the mountain is lime, laid down hundreds of millions of years ago when this land was the floor
of a great inland sea. Later, when the land fractured and
pushed up to form the Rocky Mountains, we find this same
limestone deposit on the top of the range. The vein or
fissure, or more properly speaking the fault in the formation, showed alternating layers of lime and quartzite to a
depth of two hundred feet. Below this level the earth's
history is further revealed by occasional layers of granite
which interweave between the lime and quartzite. The
gold-bearing quartz often included galena, iron, and copper
pyrites and was very rich, often assaying as much as thirty-
five dollars a ton.

Today the London Mines are visited only by the occasional hiker or Jeep driver who chooses to cross historic
old Mosquito Pass on the way to or from Leadville.

The North London mill and some cabins. Nearby is the road over Mosquito Pass

Settlement at the South London

27.

MAGNOLIA

THE GOLD BOOM that brought Magnolia into being occurred relatively later than the gold excitement just over the hill in Gilpin County. The year 1875 saw the first of many later to be erected cabins being put up near the top of the steep hill that springs sheer from above Middle Boulder Creek. Taking its name from this geographical circumstance, the region came to be known as the Big Hill mining district.

Founding father of the community was a man named Hiram Fullen, who made the initial discovery here in June as he had, two years earlier, at nearby Sunshine. After the turn of the century, a cyanide mill of fifty tons capacity was constructed to extract the gold float from such mines as the Lady Franklin, Mountain Lion, and Keystone. The Keystone was a large and complete operation, including its own residences and a boardinghouse. It was nearly a separate city in its own right. A hoist house, wheel, shaft superstructure, and several buildings still stand at the site about a mile below Magnolia.

Midway between Boulder and Nederland, on State Highway 119, is the starting point for the Magnolia road. Almost directly across from it is another steep dirt road going northwest to Sugarloaf. The Magnolia road goes southwest for two miles in a series of sharply angled climbing turns. Just prior to reaching the town, a dirt trail branches left beside a battered sign with the name "Keystone" painted on it. A hundred yards or so down this road are the ruins of the

Keystone Mine and its buildings. Another mile up the original road is Magnolia. Several cabins, some of them of twentieth-century vintage, stand at the townsite barely below the crest of the hill. Nearby, along the road, are several mine shafts and empty foundations. During the summer months a number of the cabins will be occupied. A Jeep is not essential here since the road has a good dirt surface. If followed beyond Magnolia, it comes out above Wondervu and Pinecliff on State Highway 72.*

---

* In this same area see also Gold Hill and Wall Street.

Magnolia, above Boulder Canyon, with many of its cabins converted for summer use

Abandoned workings and power winch of the Keystone Mine below Magnolia

The seven dilapidated cabins at Middleton, up the Animas Canyon from Silverton

28.

MIDDLETON

SITUATED at the base of Middle Mountain, two miles above Howardsville, is a cluster of completely abandoned cabins, sitting astride both sides of State Highway 110. If in doubt, consult the United States Forest Service map, since there are other cabins here and there along the way. At the point where Maggie Gulch enters the Animas Valley was the site of Middleton. Eureka is two or three miles north on the same road.

While rich claims were being worked all around it during the seventies and eighties, prospectors showed little interest in what was later to become Middleton. In 1893, the year that silver was demonetized by repeal of the Sherman Silver Purchase Act, two prospectors of German extraction made the first discovery. Nearly a hundred claims were laid out but the location was too close to the already established residence centers of Howardsville, Silverton, and Eureka. Consequently, very few people chose to live in Middleton and those who did soon gravitated to the other towns, despite the presence of several good-paying mines such as the Kittimac and Golden Nugget. By the early 1900's Middleton had been abandoned.*

By 1980 the mill and one of the cabins had deteriorated. One other, cabin still stands.

* In this same area see also Animas Forks, Eureka, Gladstone, Howardsville and Mineral Point.

29

MINERAL POINT

THIS WAS one of the largest and most prominent of all the many San Juan mining camps that grew up during the 1870's. The source of wealth was Mineral Point Mountain which contained a sixty-foot-thick vein of quartz with many promising veins that diverged from it. As a result, numerous mines served the camp and large quantities of silver ore were hauled to Animas Forks, or sometimes out over lofty Engineer Pass and down the nineteen-mile stagecoach route to Lake City for reduction. Assays ran from one hundred to seven hundred dollars a ton. Many of the best claims were owned by and operated for Chicago capitalists.

The town itself was first called Mineral City and consisted of the Boots and Company General Store, a sawmill, a number of restaurants, the Perry Saloon and Hotel and the customary number of log cabins. Every reference to Mineral Point refers to the fact that the town was nicknamed the "Apex of the Continent." This was probably due to the fact that it was adjacent to the source of both the Animas and the Uncompahgre rivers, close to the top of the range. The town's population usually averaged around two hundred persons and the community was served by the stagecoach line from both sides. Fare from Lake City to the east was three dollars and from Animas Forks, three miles west, the ride cost only fifty cents.

It is not easy to find Mineral Point and there's little to be seen there once you have arrived. This was formerly the highest town in San Juan County and its location doomed it to an early extinction. The altitude here is 11,474 feet, situated in an open valley near the crest of Engineer Pass. The town is located at timberline on Mineral Point Mountain, on the western slope of the Uncompahgre Range.

Three possible roads will take you to Mineral Point. The latter parts of all three are suitable only for Jeeps or hikers. The easiest of these involves a drive up State Highway 110 from Silverton, through Howardsville and Eureka to Animas Forks. As you approach the latter town, stay along the right side of the river on the trail that passes above the town. Go straight ahead past the intersection that leads up to Cinnamon Pass, over a section of slide-rock as you climb gradually up toward Engineer Pass. Where the trail bisects in two places, take the left branch in both instances.

Mineral Point lies just beyond the next knoll in a somewhat swampy meadow ringed by stunted pine trees. The crumbling remains of a mine, a few sun-bleached cabins and a dozen or so stone foundations distributed at random over the clearing are all that remain of the camp. If this same road is followed, it drops sharply down over a series of narrow ledge switchbacks until it ultimately intersects with the Million Dollar Highway just a few miles south of Ouray. This road, when followed up in reverse from Ouray, is a good and perhaps the shortest of the three trails to Mineral Point.

The route to Ouray is one of the most rugged and picturesque of the San Juan trails. In the seven miles traversed, the average descent is 547 feet to the mile, and in some places one thousand feet, with yawning chasms first on one side of the canyon wall and then on the other. So deep and fearful, it makes one shudder at the thought long after passing over the route, where one misstep would be the last on earth and the beginning of a descent into an awful abyss. The wagon road between Mineral Point and Ouray, although only seven miles in length, was three years in building. It runs along on the top of the canyon wall, in many places overlooking the fearful gorge below, affording views of varied scenery at once grand, rugged, wild, and beautiful beyond description. In this great canyon is the source of the Uncompahgre River, fed by Bear, Red, and numerous small creeks, some of which reach it in cascades, in one instance one of one hundred feet in one unbroken fall.

The third way crosses Engineer Pass from Lake City. Take the trail to the right as you come down off the top of the pass. This will lead you by some mine buildings before crossing the meadow into Mineral Point.

The demonetization of silver spelled out the death of the town and by 1899 the last of the residents had moved away.*

By 1980 the deterioration of the San Juan Chief mill was more advanced, but little else had changed.

---

* In this same area see also Animas Forks, Eureka, Capitol City, and Rose's Cabin.

Library, State Historical Society of Colorado
Montezuma's main street in 1880

The bleached bones of once rich Mineral Point, high in the San Juan-Uncompahgres

The main street of Montezuma, looking north toward Loveland Pass

30.

MONTEZUMA

MONTEZUMA is located at an altitude of 10,200 feet and lies in a beautiful little valley on the south fork of the Snake River in Summit County. The town is surrounded by rugged forest-clad mountains that rise to heights of twelve and thirteen thousand feet. Collier Mountain is on the east, Teller and Glacier on the south, Bear on the west, and Lenawee to the north.

A miner named John Coley made prospecting trips through South Park, then over the pass at the head of Bear Creek to Glacier Mountain. In 1863 he uncovered what is often referred to as the first silver discovery in the territory of Colorado. No one knew where Coley went until, after one of his trips, he showed silver ingots in Georgetown. He had smelted his ore in a crude furnace with a flue built from a hollow log, pieced with rocks and clay taken from the lode for mortar.

Shortly after Coley's discovery, miners began flocking into the region and prospecting became more general. In 1865 Edward Guibor built a cabin in what was later called Saints John. He prospected on Glacier Mountain and located both the Glacier and the Herman mines.

These discoveries started a new cycle of events and resulted in the establishment of many substantial settlements in a long belt extending down the mountains from Caribou at the northern end through Saints John, Alma, and Rosita to Silverton, Lake City, and Ouray in the silvery San Juan and Uncompahgre Mountains.

This general overoptimism about silver mining resulted in the founding of many little communities around a single mine which could not long support the swarms of silver-hungry prospectors. Most of the "boom towns" withered and died within a year or two of the time they had sprouted and blossomed. Montezuma was not one of these, and it is a good example of a town that survived its boom and still has a small permanent population.

Montezuma was founded as a mining camp in 1865. The settlement was named for the last Aztec emperor of Mexico.

It reached its peak population in 1890 when it boasted of 743 persons. It had two stores, a post office, two hotels (the Summit House and the Rocky Mountain House), a sawmill, and in later years a smelter. Prior to acquisition of the smelter, like many other silver camps, Montezuma sent its refractory ores elsewhere for refining. In the early days of silver mining Swansea, in Wales, was the best and for many sections the only place where the silver could be separated from the lead ores with which it was associated.

At that time Montezuma was described as being fourteen miles north of Webster, and a fare of three dollars was charged for the ride over Post Road No. 40.

The following article from the July 3, 1880, issue of the *Colorado Miner* (Georgetown) is interesting in the light of more recent history which has seen Montezuma outlast both the towns on which it was supposed to be dependent.

Montezuma is dependent, metaphorically speaking, upon the crumbs that fall from Chihuahua's table. Chihuahuaites have come to Montezuma to invest as the Belle and Blanche lodes are now owned and being worked by representatives from the town. Many visitors upon seeing the many deserted cabins in and around Montezuma naturally infer it is as a result of failure of the mines in that locality. These houses are inhabited by workmen employed by the Saints John Mining Company. In fact Montezuma was supported and dependent on this community.

With the drop in the price of silver the town's fortunes

declined. There was a slight revival of mining interest in 1940, but little has been done since World War II.

A total of five fires have swept the town thus far. Conflagration number four occurred in August of 1949, with damages estimated at about $20,000. The fire broke out in the building housing the general store, poolroom and tavern. This structure was built in the 1880's and was destroyed in about an hour. Sparks set fire to an adjoining building, one of the first log structures in the town. It was being used as a dwelling. Another old log barn, used for storage of sheep-herding supplies, was the third building destroyed.

Montezuma was most recently ravaged by flames just prior to Christmas of 1958, and on December 18 the *Denver Post* carried the following account:

> Fire again completed its destruction in less than two hours after it broke out in the rear of the Summit House Hotel. Cause of the fire hasn't been determined. The hotel was burned to the ground as were the town hall, three garages that belonged to the hotel, two residences, and three private garages. First to go was the hotel. Fifteen persons registered in the hotel at the time all escaped without injury. The town hall, a small frame structure and a landmark of the town, was the next to go. From there it went to residences. The last place the fire passed was the garages.

In recent years, when the town seemed nearly on its last legs, workers from the nearby Roberts Tunnel have taken up residence in Montezuma in order to be closer to their work.

Montezuma is seventy-four miles from Denver, and it cannot truly be classified as a ghost town in the ordinary sense. Its inclusion here is due to the fact that several of its original buildings, many now unoccupied, still line the main street; and because Montezuma is the starting point to go to two other locations, Saints John and the Wild Irishman Mine, both of which are definitely ghost towns, measured by any standard.

Montezuma is reached by driving in the six miles on a

good dirt road known locally as State Highway 294, which runs south from the western end of Loveland Pass. The road climbs gradually until it reaches the foot of Glacier Mountain, west of the Snowy Range and across from the south branch of the Snake River. This is the location of Montezuma, a mining town that still remains active and vital.*

By the late 1970's another fire had destroyed the hotel and a few other structures, but much remains to be seen.

---

* In this same area see also Saints John and the Wild Irishman.

31.

MOUNT FALCON

JOHN BRISBEN WALKER, the founder and owner of *Cosmopolitan Magazine,* was the first man to seek a summer White House in Colorado. This was his plan in 1910, but the project was never completed. Today the foundation of the house, which was struck by lightning and burned, is all that is left. In Denver, Walker once went into great detail explaining his plans. He said there would be two buildings, one the President's home, and, a short distance away, the President's study.

Walker hired J. B. Benedict, a Denver architect, to design the summer White House and the resulting plans were for an imposing castle of gray granite, similar to those in Central Europe. The cornerstone of Colorado yule marble was laid in 1914, and dignitaries arrived from both east and west for the ceremony.

The plans have since been characterized by other architects as being among the most spirited conceptions of mountain architecture ever produced in this country.

With these plans Walker proposed to build a massive mansion of native stone, instead of granite, quarried out of the ledges near the site of the building and contrasting with the natural setting. At last ground was broken. The proposed house was to be unique in many ways. It was to be flanked on all four corners with towers and battlements, giving it the effect of the feudal castles which overlooked the Rhine River in the Middle Ages. The house would also provide room for the President's attendants, and automobiles would bring the summer home within forty minutes of Denver.

Mr. Walker's curious means of financing the President's home was to have every school child in the United States contribute a dime. A considerable sum raised by this method was placed on deposit in an Eastern bank.

Listeners were often impressed by Mr. Walker's enthusiasm about the view, the plains to the north and east, the mountains to the south. The view to the southeast is cut off by Mount Morrison, so Mr. Walker said, "Some day I'm going to cut the top off of that mountain." He really meant that.

The view from the site, according to the building committee, was one of its strongest features. From the north terrace of the mountain on which the drawing room was to be, the view opened on the steep mountainside wooded with pines and dropped down two thousand feet to the rushing waters of Bear Creek to the north. Seventy-five miles away stood Pikes Peak. Denver lies fifteen miles off to the northeast. A yawning fireplace 1,500 feet above Cattle Rustler's Gulch juts into space, space that was once Mr. Walker's beloved lower room where he used to retire to study and write, carrying on the work he had done for many years.

Walker had the backing of William G. Evans and other civic leaders. President William Howard Taft, when told of the plan, expressed the opinion that no locality could offer finer natural attractions for such a structure. It was an excellent place for Cabinet meetings, being midway between Puget Sound and the Gulf of Mexico, the Great Lakes and Southern California. The cornerstone was made out of yule marble and was exhibited at Seventeenth and Stout in Denver in 1911 before being laid at the site.

During the latter phases of World War I, it was nearly forgotten until lightning struck and nearly destroyed the Walker castle in 1918.

From that time on work on the summer White House was at a standstill. Walker felt it was a civic responsibility to complete it, but the city fathers had other ideas. He urged in 1913 that Denver spend a million dollars in advertising to bring tourists to the West. His idea was pooh-poohed. In 1924 he offered to sell the park of the Red Rocks to Denver for a fraction of its worth, but his offer was turned down. He later lost the park, which was taken over by the city. The solid stone work in the reconstruction of the castle was done by imported foreign laborers and included eight fireplaces, which made five in the main house and three in the servant's quarters. On a knoll back of the house Walker ordered a race track built and here trotters wheeled their carts about for crowds that came up from Denver. To encourage visitors to enjoy his mountain paradise, Walker built a twisting auto road up Mount Falcon in 1911. The road has a 12 per cent grade and, impossible as it seems, was used for races.

It began to look as if the long-projected summer home for the President would finally be erected on the summit of Mount Falcon, and a movement was launched by a special committee of the Denver Civic and Commercial Association. In order to raise fifty thousand dollars, the amount necessary to complete the main building, a resolution was passed. Later embellishments were to be added to the building at a cost of $250,000. The actual work of obtaining the money depended upon the tender by the city of a contract and deed by which Mr. Walker was to transfer to Denver a hundred acres of Mount Falcon to be added to the Mountain Parks on condition that the city would build a graded road to the branch from either the Bear Creek or the Turkey Creek roads and proceed to the top of the mountain.

According to the *Rocky Mountain News* of June 12, 1914, President Wilson was to be at the ceremony to lay the cornerstone and tremendous crowds were expected to attend. One of the three roads was to be used for motor-driven vehicles, one for horse-drawn conveyances and the third for the return of all classes of traffic to Denver. Mrs. Woodrow Wilson and the entire presidential family were sent special invitations to attend the ceremony as guests of the Inter Mountain Country Club at Morrison, Colorado.

But President Wilson got only as far as Denver. Nevertheless, after an impressive ceremony led off by Stanley Steamers the stone was finally laid on Mount Falcon on the Fourth of July, 1914, but hard times, lack of public interest, and most of all the lack of an atom bomb to frighten Washington into decentralizing, doomed the castle. These misfortunes did the project in and fire finished what had been started, leaving only a druid ruin on Mount Falcon. The cornerstone was hauled off to the Mount Morrison Hotel. The noble and massive structure, two thousand feet above Bear Creek and only forty minutes from Denver, stood alone.

Today the long living room with its five fireplaces and the servants' house with its three fireplaces and the patio are all still discernible, but it was never visited by a President.

In the 1970's Walker's Castle became a Jefferson County park. Clearly marked signs now line the highway between Kittredge and Indian Hills, directing you to Mt. Falcon Park. From the parking circle a new, shorter hiking path from the west takes you to the ruins.

Library building at the President's home on Mount Falcon

Druid ruins of the Walker castle, built as a summer White House atop Mount Falcon

32.

NEVADAVILLE

COLORADO owes much to Gilpin County. Around its decaying buildings and abandoned mines cluster the romance of the early days and the story of the development of an empire. It was a place of strong men and its gold laid the foundations of the state. Black Hawk and Central City are well known. Nevada City, as it was first called, though only a mile or so up the hill, was less familiar and is now deserted most of the time. Nevadaville's post office was named Bald Mountain since the postal department said there was already a Nevadaville elsewhere and another would simply compound the confusion. Stubborn miners failed to accept the change and continued to call their community Nevadaville. The town is located on Bald Mountain, on the north side of Nevada Gulch, and this was the source of the name assigned it by the postal department. Directly south across the gulch is Quartz Hill, a virtual series of pitfalls, rocks, and prospect holes. Visitors to the region could ride the Colorado division of the Union Pacific Railroad up from Denver to Central City for $3.10. From there they were on their own since no regular conveyance ran up the hill from Central City to Nevadaville.

Nevadaville is one of the oldest mining towns of Colorado. The famous Burrows lode was discovered in 1859, just after the discovery of the big Gregory mine near Central City. Water was a big problem until 1860 when a ditch was made that brought water from Peck Gulch in North Clear Creek from about eight miles away.

The town had hardly put down its roots to achieve a start when the usual tragedy struck. The *Rocky Mountain News* reported the event on November 7, 1861.

The Conflagration In and About Nevadaville

Many people have lost their houses and household goods and, at the same time, were thrown out of employment for the coming winter. There was no damage done on Eureka Street except for the burning of a few cabins at the end of Prosser Gulch.

The fire has died out. It originated above the city in the timber. It was first discovered on Monday A.M. about 8 o'clock. By noon it was down in the city. The principal part of the town was burned out. Whitcomb's mill was the only one burned. The building was a total loss. Machinery was not entirely destroyed, but they had 600 cords of wood burned. Merchants, hotel keepers, and saloon keepers in Central City moved their goods into prospect holes and tunnels. The next morning they were all busy carrying them back again. One merchant had $600 worth of clothing stolen and Jack Langrishe did not play that nite or the next. Fifty houses worth $60,000 went up in flames.

Four months later, the *News* again wrote about Nevadaville and described it as follows:

A part of the town system that begins with Black Hawk, Mountain City, Central City, and ends up here. It's a puzzle to a stranger to tell where one town begins and another ends, not withstanding the fact that there are three distinct corporations. Nevadaville is at the very door of a number of the great mines and is essentially the home of the miners. On the other side and above the stamp mill are to be seen the cozy homes made happy by the husband's toil beneath the surface. Like its neighbor, this town is also improving with a handsome brick block, the walls of which are almost completed, that is soon to adorn Main Street. No signs of poverty or want are to be seen. The laborer gets almost as much here for a day's work as he could in Massachusetts for a week's toil.

In 1864 the town had a population of six thousand. One of the citizens was the famous Pat Casey, an illiterate Irish miner who became wealthy from the rich Casey Mine above the town. Numerous amusing Pat Casey stories are still told in Gilpin County.

Nevadaville is thirty-eight miles west of Denver and may

be reached by three different roads, none of them particularly difficult or hazardous. The most direct and obvious road leaves Central City at the large parking lot and goes right up the rather steep valley for something over a mile. This route leads directly into Nevadaville.

The second way begins at Central City at the same spot, following past the parking lot, then up around the hairpin curves that are the Virginia Canyon road. Upon reaching the large mine on your left, where signs concerning the glory hole are prominently displayed, take the road that switches back sharply to your right and go up to the glory hole. From here, merely follow the road over the crest of Quartz Hill, from which point Nevadaville may be seen in the valley below you. The road, rough in spots, continues down across the creek and on into the town.

The third route involves following Eureka Street in Central City to the top of the hill where the several cemeteries are located. At this point the second road from your left should be taken. It will lead you around behind Bald Mountain, through lush alpine meadows filled with a profusion of variously colored wild flowers, then back down into the valley where Nevadaville's dozen or so buildings still stand.*

In the 1970's some restoration work was done on existing structures. Nevadaville is well worth seeing.

* In this same area see also American City, Apex, and Nugget.

The abandoned site of once busy and prosperous Nevadaville, showing the Masonic Hall on the main street. The picture was taken from Quartz Hill.

This McClure photograph of Nevadaville was made in a happier day from atop Quartz Hill.

33.

NINETY FOUR

SOME CITIES are named for rivers, mountains, or other natural geographical features. Many communities have been named for their founders, for sweethearts back home, or in honor of a notable person. Sometimes names are taken from inanimate objects like "Horseshoe" or "Nugget," and not infrequently the choice has been prompted by patriotic or religious motives. Ninety Four was different, taking its calling from a numerical basis because it was founded in 1894. One thing led to another and a surprising burst of originality resulted in the prime producing property being named the Ninety Four Mine. Somehow the nearby Lalla and Princess Alice mines escaped the blight and were given more conventional names. All three contributed to the financial basis of the camp.

In reality, Ninety Four was never formally incorporated, and some doubt exists as to whether or not it even had a post office. Here was another example of a small mining community that grew up in the form of a cluster of buildings around the principal mining property. A few of the structures were of conventional log construction while others were built from the more traditional dressed lumber. One of the latter still sports a fair coat of white paint. To some extent, the life of the camp was merged with the town of Alice, a mile below and slightly southwest, while Yankee Hill was just another mile up over the crest of the hill. This very nearness to older, more established camps probably precluded the success of any separate civic designation. The townsite was literally hacked out of the steep side of Yankee Hill and limited space alone would have discouraged any really serious growth.

The view from Ninety Four is an interesting one. Straight west, across the canyon, the nearly complete expanse of the Forest Service hiking trail to St. Mary's Glacier can be seen, along with the glacier itself and the surrounding peaks. Off to the south in the distance are additional ranges, dominated by 14,000-foot Grays and Torreys peaks.

Drive up State Highway 285, the Fall River canyon road, from U.S. 6 and 40 just west of Idaho Springs. Follow this road to Alice along the way to St. Mary's Glacier. About twenty-five yards beyond the intersection at Alice you will see a steep, narrow and rocky trail going up to the right of the road. Cross the ditch and follow this trail to Ninety Four. There are two forks in the trail; go right at the first and keep left when you reach the second. The town is barely beyond the second fork. The other branch leads across the ridge on a wild Jeep ride to Central City.*

---

* In this same area see also Alice.

The principal street of Ninety Four. St. Mary's Glacier would be just out of the picture at the left.

Workings and cabins at Ninety Four. Picture is taken looking southwest

34.

NORTH STAR

THE NAME of this town has long intrigued me as being about the most picturesque title any community could want. It was first called Lake's Camp and was established in 1878. Largest producer was the North Star Mine, located the following year. Actually the town was built on the property of the May Mazeppa Mine at the southern edge of Whitepine. Its life span was typical of Colorado silver camps and paralleled those of nearby Tomichi and Whitepine, embracing a characteristic boom in the eighties and a bust after the silver crash of '93, which left the town deserted in the usual pattern.

As you enter the town, after the road bends around, the first building at your left will be a large white false front, the Leadville House. The log structure beyond it has been called the post office. Across the road, which someone with a remarkable stroke of originality named Main Street, are two more cabins.

The road, or more properly the trail, to North Star runs northeast from the south edge of Whitepine. It is accessible only through the May Mazeppa property and local permission must be secured to avoid trespassing. In order to insure conformity, a strong steel cable with a unique padlock arrangement spans the trail at the lower end. The distance up from this point is only a mile, but the grade is a climbing one all the way. In places the stone cribbing is visible along both sides of the path which, incidentally, follows Galena Gulch. This cribbing is the only real danger, aside from the customary roughness encountered on unused trails.

The gulch road is a very narrow one, and travel here would not be advisable for vehicles as wide as most contemporary cars since the restrictive width leaves no room for the driver to turn out around sharp rocks or to avoid scraping the high centers. As a Jeep road, though, it's not even mildly exciting. At the top is a good wooden bridge to be crossed, then the trail bends left, past the flagpole, and you're in North Star.*

By 1980 the old hotel's sagging was more pronounced, but little else had changed.

* In this same area see also Tomichi and Whitepine.

35.

NUGGET

BY THE TIME Nugget came into being in the latter part of the 1890's, its chances of survival alongside nearby Apex, American City, Kingston, Central City, and other already established centers was limited to say the least. Technically speaking, its location on the outer fringes of the booming Pine Creek mining district left a lot to be desired. By this late date, many of the miners who entered Gilpin County did so with their pockets already full of glittering dust when they left home, only to face starvation in the severe winters after their arrival. In many instances they ate the oxen which carried them over and then lived on bullrushes for weeks at a time. In this country, those who went out hunting after their arrival often got lost and starved to death. Such conditions were a hazard that had to be faced in the camps like Nugget that grew up so far off the beaten path.

So little remains of the early town of Nugget that its exact location has been something of a local mystery in some quarters. A few scattered buildings and a huge old mine on the hillside above it are all that mark its place in the sun today.

If you want to see it, follow instructions for going to Apex and American City. Go on north toward James Peak, past the cutoff to American City and down the fairly steep grade. At the foot of the hill, take the first left turn. Follow this trail about one hundred yards or so and the remains of Nugget are nestled there among the dense shrubbery.

Watch the oil pan and muffler on this one since the natural drainage has left a rather high center in several spots.

Nugget was a one-mine camp with little in the way of civic development to assure a measure of permanence. No church was ever constructed, and even the ch'ldren had to trudge up the hill for a weary two miles to attend school at nearby American City. It must have been a dreary place in which to live. Even at this altitude, the mosquitoes and their noisy relatives are very thick at Nugget during the summer months. In winter, a thick blanket of snow covers the bottom of the valley where the cabins are, and traces of it remain well into June. With such obstacles as these to overcome, the impermanence of camps such as Nugget is understandable.*

---

* In this same area see also American City, Apex, and Nevadaville.

Looking down on Nugget's two cabins from the abandoned mine shaft on the hill above the town.

North Star, scattered among the trees in a high alpine meadow above Whitepine

36.

OLD OPHIR

THROUGHOUT the latter part of the mining period, two towns called Ophir existed just a short distance apart. Both towns derived their names from mention in the Old Testament of a region said to be the source of gold. Another version holds that the towns were named for the adjacent Ophir needles, an unusually beautiful series of rock formations on the hillside north of the town, which in turn derived their names from the Biblical location. Going from the sublime to the ridiculous, there is an illogical and somewhat profane third version explaining the choice of the name.

By almost any standards, Old Ophir is Colorado's newest ghost town, despite the fact that it was first founded in the 1870's and antedates New Ophir. Several new twentieth century frame homes were constructed here following the conclusion of World War II to house workers for a mining project that failed to prosper. Still in excellent condition, these homes now stand vacant along the main street. The peak population during the boom years was only five hundred, but it has never been completely deserted. Each year, some people still return, imbued with the unshakable idea that rich pockets of ore are still undiscovered in the area.

Ophir is accessible over two widely different routes. From a point about three miles west of Telluride, State Highway 145 becomes a good dirt road and runs south to Rico. Twelve miles south of the intersection is New Ophir. From here an undesignated dirt road runs straight east for two miles to Old Ophir, built in the middle of a meadow. If you have a Jeep, drive on east through the town and up over Ophir Pass, a thrilling shelf road, steep and narrow, cut entirely from the slide-rock. An eerie and frightening effect results as the cleated tires churn up the slide-rock and hurl pieces over the sheer edge of the shelf. Pause at the top for a magnificent view of the San Miguel Valley far below you. Ophir Pass was first opened as a toll road for wagons in 1881 and was reopened for Jeeps in the last decade. From the top the trail winds leisurely down the eastern slope, over Burro Bridge, to intersect with U.S. 550, the Million Dollar Highway, just a few miles north of Silverton. From Silverton this route can be followed in reverse to Ophir but the effect is not as thrilling.*

* Also in this same area see Alta.

Old Ophir, Colorado's newest ghost town. The grade up Ophir Pass is visible on the peak at the left rear.

How ghostly can a ghost town get? Some foundations and the railroad grade through Quartz.

37.

QUARTZ

THE TOWN called Quartz was started in 1879 at a point about seven miles north of Pitkin, just before moving up Cumberland Pass and going on over the top to reach Taylor Park and the town of Tin Cup. Just across the range to the east a wild Jeep road follows the old right-of-way of the Denver, South Park and Pacific Railway to the Alpine Tunnel, Williams Pass, or Alpine Pass. No matter which route you take, all three eventually join up at Hancock on the other side of the range.

This was a carbonate camp and ores recovered here showed a heavy concentration of carbonate of lead. A short distance north of the townsite on the east side of the road you can still see the remains of one of the old mills that presumably was used to refine the precious ore brought out of the mines nearby.

Quartz is located on State Highway 162. A few stone foundations on the right side of the road, just beyond the mound of earth that formerly held the railroad tracks through the town, are the remains which mark the site. About twenty-five yards beyond this point, going toward Cumberland Pass, are two cabins in a doubtful state of repair and situated on the opposite side of the road. A new bridge was constructed over Quartz Creek in the 1970's and some new homes have been built.

* In this same area see also Hancock, Romley, St. Elmo, Tin Cup, and Woodstock.

38.

QUERIDA

THE TOWN of Querida, in Custer County, began in June of 1877 when a former sailor named E. G. Bassick turned to mining and located an unusual mineral deposit in the Wet Mountain Valley some two miles north of Rosita. The discovery took the form of a chimney or round deposit of ore from six to twenty-five feet in width. The ore consisted of galena, zinc blend, gray copper, and tellurides of gold and silver, fluoride of silver and free gold. He named the claim for himself and a town called Bassickville grew up around it. The name was later changed to Querida. The town had its own post office, sawmill, smelter, a few stores, and a population of five hundred persons.

There were quite a number of good paying mines in the vicinity and several others showed as good prospects as the Bassick at the surface. In the early days there was no regular conveyance to bring visitors into the town, but there were connections to Rosita and to Silver Cliff, four miles east.

The Bassick Mine was often described as putting out something over 500 tons of ore a week and yielding $200,000 per month. Visitors were not allowed to come to the mine and its fabulous richness was kept a secret from the public. The mine was subsequently sold to an Eastern syndicate and is said to have produced ore valued at about $20,000,000.

Mining was not the only industry in the valley. Over 200,000 tons of hay were shipped out of the Wet Mountain

Valley by railroad each season, and also a large crop of potatoes in excess of the home demand.

To reach Querida today, follow State Highway 67 south from Florence to the intersection with State 96, which may be followed west to Querida. Another route follows Texas Creek south from State Highway 50. This is State 69. Turn east onto State 96 at Westcliffe, through Silver Cliff to Querida. No Jeep is necessary for this trip.*

Some additional deterioration was noted in 1979, but most cabins are still as described.

* In this same area see also Bent's Stockade and Rosita.

Cabins and the huge dump of the once rich Bassick Mine at Querida

39.

RED MOUNTAIN TOWN

RED MOUNTAIN TOWN was a silver camp that sprang to life following 1879 when some small silver deposits were discovered in the high alpine meadow that clings precariously to the slopes of Red Mountain. First called Sky City, the town was moved at least once from its original location on Congress Hill before settling down to some degree of permanence at its present location. Most of the stories we get concerning the earlier locations refer to it as Old Congress Town or Congress Town. These versions usually go on to tell how it moved up the hill two or three different times to eventually become Red Mountain Town. Despite this, the Colorado Business Directory for 1884 lists both towns separately and shows a population of forty for Congress and two hundred for Red Mountain Town. One story has it that when Slover and Wright moved their saloon, the whole thirsty population just naturally followed along in order to be close to their tower of strength.

The first prospectors arrived while deep snow still covered Red Mountain Park and the waves of population continued to arrive during the early 1880's. An elevation of 11,300 feet should have been anything but conducive to the founding of a town; but rich mines such as the Enterprise, Congress, Summit, and National Belle continued to attract new migrants to the district.

The National Belle was one of the first to be discovered and was a perpetually rich producer throughout the life of the town. Its tall, angular shaft house has somehow survived the several fires that plagued the town and it still sits proudly atop its yellowed mine dump at the north side of the meadow. Worst of the several destructive fires that raked the camp occurred in 1892 and left about half of the surface buildings in a shambles. The most recent began as a forest fire in 1938 and nearly finished the job.

In 1883, when the boom really slipped into high gear, Otto Mears built one of his amazing toll roads over Red Mountain to serve the needs of the area and of Mr. Mears. One of the West's most remarkable characters, Mears was born in Russia in 1841. Orphaned at the age of four, he made his way to this country and began his new life in San Francisco with the sum of less than a dollar in his pocket. From this inauspicious beginning he proceeded to parlay an active imagination and his capacity for visionary achievement into a railroad and toll-road empire in southwestern Colorado that earned him the nickname of "Pathfinder of the San Juans."

The arrival of his new road seems a more likely reason for moving the town to its present location than the saloon episode. The road was used constantly but was not adequate for the booming volume of business. In June of 1887, Mears began construction of his narrow-gauge "Rainbow Route" from Silverton, over Red Mountain Pass, finally reaching the town, a mile below the top, in September of the following year. It passed directly below the National Belle. There are some fine old photographs that are occasionally published.

The population of Red Mountain Town may have reached one thousand, according to one estimate. There were various lodges, private clubs, a school, and a local of the miners' union there; but no church was ever included.

Several newspapers flourished at various times during the life of the camp and nearly a hundred businesses of many kinds prospered in the town. Severe winters with deep snows depleted the population and slowed output of the mines. As with most silver camps, its nemesis was the year 1893.

Drive north from Silverton or south from Ouray on U.S. 550, the Million Dollar Highway, to the crest of 11,018-foot-high Red Mountain Pass. Barely below the top on the north side, about one mile, a small dirt road leaves the pavement and runs east for about a quarter of a mile to a hollow meadow behind the knoll you will see from the highway. There, spread out below you, are the scarred streets, cabins, and workings of Red Mountain Town.*

In 1980 the jail was gone and most other buildings were collapsed.

---

* In this same area see also Ironton, Mineral Point, and Sneffels.

The National Belle Mine, at left, sits like a sentinel above
the scattered ruins of Red Mountain Town.

A few of the remaining cabins at the last site of Red Mountain Town

40.

ROMLEY

SITUATED in a high alpine meadow near the source of Chalk Creek are the several old buildings that remain on the site of once bustling and busy Romley. Prior to assuming its present name, the town was first called Murphy's Switch, from the coincidence that placed a railroad switch on the line of the Denver, South Park and Pacific Railway at this point on its route over the divide by way of the Alpine Tunnel. According to the late Tony Stark, longtime keeper of the post office and general store at nearby St. Elmo, the Murphy in the name came from the prolonged illness of a local Irish prospector in the 1870's. While hospitalized in Denver, he became enamored of the nurse who cared for him and promised that, if he ever got well and struck it rich, he'd name a mine after her. Recover he did and the Mary Murphy Mine was the result. During the Chalk Creek boom, it employed hundreds of men and is said to have produced millions in ore. There are two other versions of the discovery of the Mary Murphy, but neither story is as colorful as the above, which may be only folklore. In 1881 this mine was the biggest bonanza on Chalk Creek and produced at the rate of $125 a ton in both gold and silver. The town grew down the slope from the mine and was built in the 1870's, although the name Romley was not adopted until 1897.

Romley was often referred to as the "red town," since all its buildings, for some unknown reason, were painted a bright red, with white trim around the doors and windows.

The road to the town is quite a good one. Drive south from Buena Vista on U.S. Highway 285 to Nathrop, turn right (west) and follow State Highway 162 to the eastern edge of St. Elmo. At this point a good dirt road takes off sharply up to your left. This road is not shown on any regular highway maps but is indicated on the one for San Isabel National Forest. Continue along this route for about five miles upward from St. Elmo. Romley will be on your right and lies cradled in a meadow below the level of the road. The mine on the left side of the roadbed, across from the town, was the Mary Murphy, still standing despite the rigors of rather severe winter snows which annually inundate the valley.

The Mary Murphy was sold a total of three times and ultimately was purchased by a British concern who operated it profitably through the second decade of the present century. As production dwindled, Romley began to die since the town was largely dependent on its output and that of the lesser Pat Murphy. With its business from the mines having declined sharply, the railroad removed its tracks in 1926 and, for all practical purposes, ended the life of Romley. Romley's remaining buildings were destroyed by the mining operation in 1982.*

---

* In this same area see also Hancock and St. Elmo.

Old post office and abandoned cabins in the meadow at Romley, the "red town." These buildings have since been destroyed by mining operations.

At Romley, the stairway that goes to nowhere

41.

ROSE'S CABIN

A HIGH, remote alpine meadow in southwestern Colorado is the site of Rose's Cabin. Up here the past is still linked strongly with the present. There has been no permanent human habitation here for many years. The place is not a town and never was. Rose's Cabin was the chief stage-coach stop on the Engineer Pass route. It was here that stage drivers changed their six horses on the way to and from Lake City or Silverton in the days before the railroad. The settlement was not unknown to either fame or history. On the topographical map of the Silverton Quadrangle, published by the United States Geological Survey, you can see the location indicated by its name, two black dashes and a dot.

The cabin was built from pine logs in 1874 by Corydon Rose. The previous year the Brunot Treaty was signed with the Utes for cession to the United States of a strip of land sixty miles wide and seventy miles long in the San Juans. A post office was established at Rose's Cabin on July 27, 1878, and Charles Scheaffer was appointed the first post-master as soon as he was able to post the proper bond. Further attention came to the district with the first discovery of rich veins nearby. Soon a store, restaurant, and a few miners' cabins appeared to care for the needs of a population of about fifty people.

Reports of mineral wealth brought additional prospectors and Rose's Cabin became a temporary haven for those who had started out from Lake City in coaches behind six horses or in spring buckboard wagons. It was served by daily stages from Lake City and Animas Forks and the fare was $2.25. When the stage pulled in, men came running out of the barn and began to unhitch the horses. If a person planned to stop here, it was a good idea to hurry inside as the cabin was nearly always filled. Rose himself always wore a long black coat, high hat, and met the traveler at the door with a hearty, "Howdy, stranger." His bar extended the full length at one side of the room for the convenience of those who chose to stand before it and celebrate their good fortune. A faro dealer in short sleeves, plush waistcoat and long flowing tie held forth at the far end of the bar. Remnants of the old bar could be seen inside until the roof caved in a few years ago. Across the room was a large iron safe with the name "Charles Scheaffer" across its top in gold letters. It's still there, rusting in the meadow alongside the cabin.

Upstairs were partitions that formed twenty-two bedrooms, equipped with beds of the spindle variety, now so sought after by lovers of antiques. Nothing remains of the interior since the great log outer walls have fallen to the ground.

In summer large amounts of ore were packed into the place on burros from the mines to the west as well as from those nearby. Rose kept a pack train of sixty animals to carry supplies to the high mines and for bringing the ores back down for later reshipment by wagon to Lake City, fifteen miles away, for reduction.

The cabin went out as a place of rest and refreshment, and as a local institution, around the turn of the century. Early in this century there were plans for making it a headquarters for extensive mining interests nearby which were being operated by the Golconda Mines Incorporated, of Indianapolis, Indiana. Later, one corner of the cabin held an emergency phone, connected to the Lake City system.

From Lake City, the road to Rose's Cabin follows Hensen

Creek, through the towns of Hensen and Capitol City. Beyond this latter point, Jeeps are essential for the last few miles to the cabin.

Weather can change quickly at this altitude. It was a beautiful day on my last trip from Rose's Cabin over Engineer Pass when, shortly after noon, the air became suddenly colder, clouds shut out the sunlight, and it was evident that a storm was brewing. With all possible haste we started on the rocky downward trail. As it was all downhill, we hoped to outtravel the storm. Angry nature fumed, fretted, and threatened for a half hour or so, and then the rain came down in torrents and all the elements seemed pretty busy for a while. Such mountain storms usually pass quickly but for sheer ferocity they must be seen to be appreciated, and proper protective clothing should always be carried at these altitudes.

The old safe disappeared in the 1970's. The roof and upper story of the stable are gone too. Currently the new trail passes above the townsite. At the fork, take the older road that goes downhill.

---

* In this same area see also Capitol City and Mineral Point.

Rose's Cabin, stage stop on the Engineer Mountain route. The original cabin is at the left, the stonework of the hotel fireplace is in the center foreground, and the old stable stands at the right.

Coxcomb, Wild Horse, and Eagles Nest peaks from the top of Engineer Mountain

42.

ROSITA

IN THE Wet Mountain Valley, southwest of Colorado Springs, lies Rosita, one of our most accessible ghost towns. Rosita was once the county seat of Custer County and is located fifty miles southwest of Pueblo, thirty miles south from Canon City, and seven miles southeast from Silver Cliff. The town's name is Spanish for "little rose." It was laid out in 1873 and its peak population consisted of 2,100 people, most of whom were engaged in mining, while others applied themselves to agriculture and stock raising. Rosita had stores of all kinds, a bank, several hotels (chief of which was the Grand View), two stamp mills, and two concentration works. A weekly newspaper, the *Sierra Journal*, carried local news as well as accounts of happenings from the outside. In 1876 the *Rosita Index*, another weekly, was published.

The easiest way to reach Rosita today is to take State Highway 115 south from Colorado Springs to Florence, then follow State Highway 67 to Wetmore and State 96 to the sign on the left directing you to Rosita. Should you miss the sign and go on to Querida, a two-mile-long dirt road cuts back to Rosita from there.

The first location at Rosita, originally called Brown's Spring, was made by Richard Irwin, founder of the town called Irwin in Gunnison County, and two companions in the summer of 1873. By 1878 the population had grown to about 1,500 but dropped off to about 1,200 in 1879.

Rosita is one of our oldest "big" towns. Along with

Denver and Leadville, it was one of the first three Colorado communities to have telephone service. The Denver and Rio Grande Railway formerly had a line into the Wet Mountain Valley through Grape Creek Canyon, just west of Rosita. According to an account in the *Canon City Record* on September 11, 1919, it was washed out during a flood in that stream about twenty-five years before. The flood was the most remarkable that ever came down Grape Creek and it entirely wiped out the railroad track and grade. Hardly a vestige of the roadbed remained a couple of hours after the freshet. The rails, torn and bent by the force of the water, were hopelessly lost in the bed of the stream. The ties were floated down on the crest of the flood and disappeared completely, many of them ultimately finding a lodging on the sand bars of the Arkansas River east of Pueblo. The railroad bridge across the river at the entrance to the Royal Gorge also gave way before the pressure of the flood and fell into the stream, a useless wreck. The Denver and Rio Grande later built into the Wet Mountain Valley from Texas Creek.

Today Rosita is a mere shadow of its former self since it was not restored after the last disastrous fire. Some time after the conflagration had subsided the following account was printed in the *Denver Tribune* for August 14, 1881:

Rosita has arisen Phoenix like from its ashes. Where six months ago stood wooden structures, now loom brick and stone. The burned district is nearly rebuilt of stone, brick, cut stone and concrete. Many new frame cottages have been put up. A new city hall has been built which also serves as a court house for Custer County. A fine appearing public school house has also been built this season and will be a graded school employing three teachers. The census shows 275 school children.

The town was nearly destroyed by this fire, which actually occured on March 10, 1881. Afterwards the town was incorporated but never fully rebuilt. The leading mines were the Senator, the Humboldt, and the Pocahontas. Production was mostly of silver and was estimated at from $1,000,000 to $1,500,000.

Despite all this, Rosita still looks more like the mind's-eye impression of what the average person thinks a ghost town should look like than almost any other except the inaccessible Carson or, possibly, St. Elmo. This coincidence results from the use of Rosita as a locale for the filming of a Technicolor wide-screen Western of recent vintage titled, "Saddle the Wind." As a result, Rosita now is being promoted as a headquarters for making Western movies. Metro-Goldwyn-Mayer moved a few old buildings closer to where the town had been, built a few new buildings to look dilapidated, and used some structures just as they stood. Fremont County boosters, where the movie makers spent their nights and money, are trying to interest more companies in further picture making. A new roof was installed on an old two-story mansion and, with the addition of a faded sign, it became a rooming house. False fronts and appropriate signs, blending beautifully with the old construction, were added to make other buildings the "Saloon" and "General Store." Hitching rails, in the finest Buck Jones tradition, stand in the street at the front of both buildings. A fine blacksmith's forge was restored and all of these pseudo-Western, Hollywood-inspired examples of early Colorado architecture are still there as of this writing.

At one time Rosita had a large brewery in addition to its own smelting and reduction works. As late as 1881 two stagecoach lines were still in operation between Rosita and Silver Cliff. Nearly every reference dealing with early Rosita has made mention of the fact that the largest cheese factory in Colorado was once located here until bovine appetites discovered the delight of nibbling at the wild garlic growing in profusion nearby. This put the cheese factory out of business.

The nearby, well-preserved cemetery contains the grave of Carl Wulsten, one of the founders of Rosita and of the earlier, ill-fated agricultural community of Colfax. It is also the last resting place of Commodore Stephen Decatur. The latter, despite persistent local rumor to the contrary, is not the famed hero of the War of 1812, but instead was a distant relative of the original Decatur who passed away in 1820, long before Rosita was founded. This latter Stephen Decatur once owned the newspaper at Georgetown, and the town of Decatur, which was situated between Georgetown and Montezuma, was named for him.

Nearby is a perlite mine which until recently provided insulation material for the Great Lakes Carbon Corporation of nearby Florence. Today this once great silver camp is doggedly fighting extinction after having successfully withstood the ravages of prospectors, politicians, the fire of the 1880's and the Hollywood of the 1950's.

Behind the town and across the valley, the Sangre de Cristo Range rises abruptly, forming a most magnificent backdrop for this now tiny ghost camp that was formerly one of Colorado's largest cities.*

Much had changed here by 1980. All principal structures have disappeared, only foundations remain.

---

* In this same area see also Bent's Stockade and Querida.

Abandoned Hollywood sets along Tyndall Street at Rosita showing the general store and saloon.

An old mansion at Rosita. Hollywood added a new roof and the "Rooms" sign

43.

RUBY-IRWIN

THE TOWNS OF Ruby and Irwin are usually spoken of as a single community since, as each expanded, they soon grew together and formally united. In 1879 the area was known as Ruby, when silver was king in Colorado. As the camp continued to grow it was renamed Irwin.

Its location, thirty miles north of Gunnison on Ruby Gulch, a mile above its junction with Coal Creek, was on a remarkable uplift of mineral territory. It became one of the most important camps in the county and the principal town in the Ruby mining district, deep in the heart of the Elk Mountains at an altitude of 10,044 feet.

The place presented many attractions for the tourist as well as the capitalist. Population was estimated at five hundred. Irwin boasted about five hundred buildings including seventy-five business firms, all doing a good business.

Irwin and its surroundings contained a great number of stores of all kinds, a stamp mill, large sampling works, six sawmills, one bank, three churches (Episcopalian, Methodist, and Presbyterian), one theater, many hotels (chief of which was the Elk Mountain House), a brass band, and a weekly newspaper called the *Pilot*. Irwin was surrounded by mining camps in the gulches and small basins among the hills where great numbers of prospectors and others worked out assessments. Besides the resources above mentioned there were numbers of mineral springs of sulphur, soda, and iron, said to possess rare medicinal properties.

The rich mineral belt that gave the camp its name covered

an area of about eighteen square miles and was surrounded on the north, east, and west by other belts where minerals used to abound in large quantities. Two thousand claims were located and recorded and about fifty were developed into good paying mines. The Ruby Chief was the first discovery, located June 5, 1879, by Brennan and Defenbaugh.

The ores were silver bearing, carrying brittle, wire horn, and native silver with arsenical iron. The most famous mines in Gunnison County were the Forest Queen, which employed eighty to one hundred men for four or five years, and the Ruby King. Both were on the same vein. One party claimed 1,500 feet northeast and the other 1,500 feet southwest. The first was located by William A. Fisher, of Maryland, and later owned by A. P. Mace, of Iowa.

A shaft sunk on the Forest Queen near the center of the claim to a depth of eighty feet passed through a continuous ore body on an average of three feet thick milling 1,089 ounces of silver with a good per cent of gold.

In addition to mining and mercantile pursuits, there was also some lumbering on the nearby hillsides.

In 1880 lots which had sold the year before at from ten to twenty-five dollars each, brought as much as five thousand dollars. By 1883, one estimate showed Irwin with a population exceeding six thousand persons. From what we know today, this was either shameless bragging or a typographical error. There just wasn't room for that many people.

In 1881 the *Gunnison Democrat* published the following lengthy but very laudatory article:

The people comprising the population of this camp are remarkable in many respects, representing every state in the Union and most every civilized country on the globe. All activated by a laudible ambition to share in the riches that nature has so lavishly deposited here.

On the shores of Lake Brennan at the foot of Ruby Peak, there was established a mining camp destined in a few months to achieve a world wide reputation for the extraordinary value and great number of its mines. The town of Irwin, as if by magic, sprang into existence. Its location is in a beautiful little valley between Elk and Anthracite Mountains, the entrance to which is guarded by that grim sentinel, Mount Carbon. While at its upper extremity, Ruby Peak and other mountains perform a light duty while seeming to enclose the city and lake in a beautiful basin, skirted by mountain streams with the coldest and purest water. Here is a cradle, guarded by nature's own protectors in the shape of mountains and forests. Here resides as fearless, energetic and hospitable a community as ever existed in any country, its business men being energetic and honorable in all they undertake. While the ladies of the city, the wives and daughters of these men are as intelligent and refined as any that ever graced an eastern drawing room.

Entering the city at the end of lower Ninth Street and passing up toward Lake Brennan one can form an idea of the wonderful amount of improvement made in the last sixteen months. For one-fourth of a mile one sees on either side of the street, business houses which for style of finish and capacity is not excelled by any town of twice the size in the west. Five blocks of business houses, two stories high and ranging from sixty to eighty feet in depth, which for neatness of finish and appointments are not surpassed, greets the visitor on every side and upon examination of the stocks kept within and of the business transacted at these houses will show that our business men understand the wants of the community.

The camp is now provided with seven sawmills and although they were run at their greatest capacity, the demand for lumber exceeded the supply. Owing to the great demand for lumber for building purposes and the abundant supply of timber, three more mills will be erected in the spring.

Professions include an excellent banking house, public reading room, newspaper, churches to make a complete settlement and life pleasant to the residents.

To friends, in states east of us we say, "If you're tired of your present condition and surroundings come to this new eldorado of the west. If you wish to live in a higher altitude, a purer atmosphere, in a healthier country with a better climate where nature has lavished wealth for all who will come to secure it; if you would live in a land high up in the clouds where you may watch the intermingling of the sunshine and shadow and enjoy a climate tempered by the commingling of summer's heat with winter's cold resulting in balmy spring where waters are purest and air most invigorating, then come here. But if you're contented and happy where you are and you expect wealth without personal effort, if you cannot endure occasional hardships and lack pluck and energy, then remain where you are.

The exclusive Irwin Club entertained Grant and Roosevelt and was a useful asset to the town as members could bring their friends and visitors either on business or socially, as distinguished men were arriving frequently during the first two or three summers. For instance, they entertained Teddy Roosevelt, who was swinging around the circle before lighting on a cattle ranch in South Dakota. He was then just a young man out of Harvard College. General Grant and most of the prominent statesmen of Colorado visited here at one time or another. As there was no lobby outside of a saloon in the town, the club was a place where members could meet friends and discuss business and social affairs. All was well until the ladies of the town spread the rumor that their husbands spent their evenings there drinking and playing poker.

When former President Grant was returning East from his round-the-world tour, he visited many Colorado mining camps. His stop at Ruby-Irwin was a gala occasion, with citizens riding out to meet him. A grand parade was staged and Grant is said to have driven his own coach into town. He stayed two days.

Ruby-Irwin was situated on the original White River Ute Indian trail and was, in fact, built on land belonging to the Utes. Fear of attack from this quarter was a constant possibility, but it failed to materialize.

The main highway over Kebler Pass, between Crested Butte and Somerset, goes within two miles to the right of the townsite. The three peaks in back of the town are Ruby, Purple, and Mount Owen.

State Highway 135 north from Gunnison through Crested Butte should be followed to reach this area. Just beyond Crested Butte and before crossing Kebler Pass, turn right and watch for the United States Forest Service sign marking the town's site. The Forest Queen Mine still sits above the meadow on a huge tailings dump and about four cabins, two of them hidden in the trees across the creek, still stand.

All the rest are gone, save for a few foundations among the willows. These foundations indicate there was once a town here but give no indication of the size and importance of Irwin.

From here you may wish to continue on up the hill to the lake, a beautiful spot where the road ends. Going back down, just beyond the intersection on the road to Kebler Pass, there is an interesting memorial commemorating the site of the town cemetery with a single grave. It has one of those priceless inscriptions so dear to the hearts of Sunday newspaper feature editors. It goes like this:

> My good friends as you pass by,
> As you are now, so once was I.
> As I am now you soon will be,
> Prepare yourself to follow me.

The cemetery was first known as Ruby Camp Cemetery in 1879 and 1880. In 1885 it was renamed Irwin Cemetery. Irwin's heyday didn't last long. The United States soon went on the gold standard and miners and businessmen looked elsewhere for a living. By 1909 Irwin was easily a ghost town.*

By 1980 the site had changed little. Some new mining has begun in the area.

---

* In this same area see also Floresta, Gothic, and Tin Cup.

The first May Company at Ruby-Irwin and the dry goods store of Reasonable Abe show in this early photo.

Looking south along the main street of Ruby-Irwin. Old pictures show buildings along both sides of this thoroughfare. The Forest Queen Mine is at the left on the hillside.

44.

ST. ELMO

WELL PRESERVED and easily accessible, St. Elmo is probably the closest thing to the tourists' impression of what a ghost town should look like. Years ago, this was the first dead town I had ever seen and I thought it was a rather attractive corpse. The town was platted four miles past Alpine on Chalk Creek in October of 1880. At the time of its incorporation, it had a population of only four hundred inhabitants who, because of the dense growth of evergreen trees at the site, named it Forest City. Due to the fact that California already had a town by the same name and because the Post Office Department did not wish to compound the confusion, the name was changed to St. Elmo. There were stores, hotels, and a newspaper called the *Mountaineer Weekly*. The South Park division of the Union Pacific and the Denver and Rio Grande operated joint tracks to St. Elmo. Mining was the principal occupation. Galena-bearing silver, gold, and copper were located nearby. Principal producers were the Mary Murphy at nearby Romley, the Molly Murphy, and the Tilden Campaign. In addition to mining and railroading, a third industry was also based at St. Elmo. This was the starting point for the Gunnison, Aspen, and Tin Cup stage lines which operated daily over the historic road across Tin Cup Pass. This route is now a rocky Jeep road.

The town probably reached its greatest growth in 1882 when it was estimated that some 1,500 or more persons lived there. While the railroad was building in 1880-81, St. Elmo drew large Saturday-night crowds made up of miners, rail-roaders, and freighters, augmented by several hundred men then working on the Alpine Tunnel.

Many of the original buildings are still there. The Stark General Store still stands, and across from it is the old city hall with its steeple. On the other side of the creek is the old schoolhouse nestled among the aspens. Religious services of all denominations were held here since there was never a church constructed at St. Elmo. Inside are many of the original desks and old texts.

Jeeps are not necessary for the trip to St. Elmo. Follow U.S. 285 south from Buena Vista to Nathrop. Turn west at this point onto State Highway 162, which follows the now abandoned bed of the Denver, South Park, and Pacific Railway up to St. Elmo. The road, though mostly unpaved, is an easy one as it ambles along past the great chalk cliffs and the former site of the historic Mount Princeton Hot Springs Hotel, now dismantled, sold, and transported else-where. There are few turnoffs, and if in doubt, follow the bed of Chalk Creek all the way to the town. The photographer and the amateur historian will both enjoy St. Elmo.*

* In this same area see also Hancock, Quartz, Romley, Tin Cup, and Woodstock.

Main street of St. Elmo, showing the typical false fronts

The general store at St. Elmo. Note the section of old boardwalk

45.

SAINTS JOHN

WE TAKE the Jeep again and this time we are whisked into a valley of scenic wonders. Fantastic turrets crowned with lofty pines tower above us, and below is the angry, foaming torrent of Saints John Creek coursing down the mountainside toward Montezuma and the Snake River.

Saints John is situated on a silver belt two miles south of Montezuma in Summit County, at an altitude of 10,800 feet. Near the town, in the heart of these cloud-capped regions, Colorado's earliest discoveries of silver were made by John Coley of Empire in 1864. Here the Boston Silver Mining Company was established to work their mines, located high up among the peaks. At first they were one hundred miles from any source of supply, and freighting in the materials often cost ten and fifteen cents a pound. The camp was shut in during the winter from the rest of the world with an uncertain and infrequent mail which later came from Montezuma by saddle. A Colonel Chandler headed the agency and Captain Sampson Ware was the superintendent. They established their company and worked their way, year after year and often at enormous cost, into the rich treasures of Glacier Mountain. Saints John had a post office, store, sawmill, assay office, and smelting furnace. At this time it had a population of a mere fifty people.

Despite the fact that the Civil War had taken many of the younger men, Saints John started growing in 1865. The community was originally called Coleyville and was the first town to be built after Montezuma that became anything more than a dream. The origin of the town's plural name has suffered from several versions. One of these was facetiously published in the *Central City Daily Register* on Friday, August 21, 1876, under the title "How They Fixed It." The report goes on to say that Saints John was named for John Collum and John the Baptist; hence, Saints John. It now seems fairly certain that the town was started by members of the Masonic order. It was named for their two patron saints, Saint John the Baptist and Saint John the Evangelist.

Although the camp was second in age, the Saints John Mine was the oldest in the district. This was a company town, most of it being built by the Boston Mining Company when they took over the mines in 1878. The Comstock lode of the Saints John Mine had previously been operated by the Boston Silver Mining Association (or Company). It was situated on the southwest face of Glacier Mountain at an estimated altitude of twelve thousand feet. The vein of the Comstock stood nearly perpendicular and varied in size. At one point it spread out to eight feet and at another it contracted to a few feet, but it maintained an average of four to five feet. At the point of greatest width there was a stratum of compact ore two feet thick upon the head wall. The same situation also existed upon its foot wall, and ore was disseminated through the intervening mass.

About 1872 the Boston Company built the most complete and up-to-date milling and smelting works available at that time. Before this the high-grade ore could not be treated here but was sent by ox team, railroad, and sailing vessel for refinement to Swansea in distant Wales. This smelter was one of the first in the state. Its machinery was shipped in from the East and the bricks came from Wales. The *Rocky Mountain News* of October 24, 1878, reported that one hundred men were employed by the Boston Company in freighting and cutting timber and burning charcoal for their smelter and reduction works. Silver-lead bullion had been turned out during the past two or three seasons.

After 1878, when the Boston Mining Company took over, building of the town was completed. There were an assay office (which is still standing, and is shown in the picture with its swaybacked roof), a company store, a two-and-a-half-story boardinghouse, a guest house, ornately trimmed homes for the superintendent and foreman, and a mess hall as well as homes for the miners and their families. Saints John boasted, with typical Boston pride, that there wasn't a saloon in the town but there was a library, with more than three hundred volumes donated by Boston friends. Eastern and foreign newspapers were sent regularly to the library from Boston.

The superintendent's home was completely furnished with Sheraton furniture, brought from the East, but he did not live in Saints John the year round. The manager of the boardinghouse took care of the home and kept it ready for his visits. In later years the Boston Mining Company disposed of its interests in Saints John. The superintendent walked out of his home, shut the doors and left the house just as it stood. It is still standing but the contents are gone. The fate of the library was the same.

Winters in Saints John were, and still are, severe. The *Rocky Mountain News* of December 14, 1871, reported that

Through the indefatiguable efforts of G. C. O'Conner, a foreman of railway laborers and a well-known plainsman, the road over the range from Hamilton to Breckenridge and Sts. John has all along been kept open and is open for travel by sleigh with freight. O'Conner kept a force of men with mule teams at work until the four feet of snow on the range has become packed and solid, making a splendid road.

In 1898 ten snowslides were counted in one morning and snow was up to the second-story windows of the boardinghouse. Families burned candles or kerosene lamps all day.

An entrance was kept open to the boardinghouse by cutting steps from the top of the snow down to the door. Another door rested on a framework. Each night the entrance, that worked on the order of a trapdoor, was closed. After each snowfall, they would go from the Clinesmith home through a connecting snowshed to the boardinghouse, then climb out a second-story window onto the crusted surface and shovel the new snow off the wooden door and frame. After digging more steps, they would reset the framework and the trapdoor was ready for use until the next storm.

To reach Saints John today, follow U.S. Highway 6 to the bottom of Loveland Pass on the western slope of the Continental Divide. From there, follow State Highway 294, unmarked at present, southeast for the six miles to Montezuma. Go right on through town and, as you reach the southeast end of Montezuma, there is a U.S. Forest Service sign on your right pointing to a trail marked "Saints John and Grizzly Gulches." Follow this trail about two miles to the town. In winter, the hike up from Montezuma on snowshoes is an invigorating experience that I recommend highly. For the camera enthusiast, Saints John, half buried in the snow, offers many rewarding compositions framed against the distant mass of Grays and Torreys peaks.

The trail to Saints John is a comparatively easy one for Jeeps and, at times, I have seen a few conventional automobiles that were able to pull the first few steep grades and negotiate about three very tight switchbacks on the narrow, rather rocky road. The town is located at the far end of a long meadow, flanked on the southeast by Glacier Mountain.

The large building at the north end of the settlement was the two-and-one-half-story boardinghouse. Next to it was the home of Captain Sampson Ware, but only its foundation remains now. Beyond it, with its roof pointing in several directions at once, is the assay office, with its oven still remarkably intact on the inside. This building also housed the three-hundred-book library from Boston. Beside the assay office and sitting back from the main street is the two-story guest house and at the end of the row is the smaller company-owned home of the mine foreman. Across the street stands what is left of the once beautiful superintendent's house. On the other side of Saints John Creek what had been the mill is a tremendous pile of rubble stacked against the steep side of Glacier Mountain. When I first visited Saints John this latter structure was still standing, but it came down during the winter of 1958. Down the valley, on the same side of the creek, stands the brick stack of the little smelter. Old photographs show houses all over the valley between the mill and the smelter and even up on the side of Glacier Mountain, but all these are gone now.

Today, only an occasional person with a fondness for Colorado's out-of-the-way places manages to reach Saints John, and each winter successive heavy snows are slowly exacting their toll of destruction on the little town at the foot of Glacier Mountain.*

Some buildings remained in 1980, but nearly half of the town is now gone.

---

* In this same area see also Montezuma and the Wild Irishman.

Townsite of Saints John showing the smelter at the right, with Grays and Torreys peaks looming up in the background.

This winter photograph of Saints John was made before the turn of the century and offers nearly the same view up the valley as in the picture above.

46.

SANTIAGO

THE ENTIRE region surrounding Santiago was first known as the East Argentine mining district back in the early prospecting days of the 1860's. Unlike most ghost camps of Colorado, Santiago never actually became a town in the ordinary sense. It consisted of a group of miners' cabins that were erected and which eventually grew into a small community around the rich Santiago Mine. It was owned by Edward Wilcox as a part of his holdings at adjacent Waldorf, which soon overshadowed Santiago.

The site began fading rapidly about the turn of the century and wavered on the brink of emptiness for some time before giving up. Even now some work is occasionally done here in the summer. Only one road will carry the occasional visitor to what remains of Santiago today. When you take it, be sure to watch out for occasional ore trucks which sometimes come plunging down around the blind curves of the narrow trail below Mount McClellan.

Follow State Highway 281 southwest up the valley from Georgetown to Waldorf. From this point two roads lead out of the town. The one that doubles back to your right toward Mount McClellan should be followed for about three fourths of a mile. At the first intersection, go left to Santiago, which is barely out of sight behind the first low ridge.*

* In this same area see also Waldorf.

Tunnel and surface buildings at Santiago. Waldorf is in the valley below

The roofless cabins of Sherman, destroyed by floods

47.

SHERMAN

SOME SAY that Sherman was named for the Union general of Civil War fame, but the more widely accepted version has its origin in the story of an Easterner with the family name of Sherman who stopped here while hunting and prospecting. He subsequently returned home and no records remain to indicate that he ever visited the town. Sherman had its beginnings in 1877 and continued to flourish through the eighties and nineties. It was constructed on the floor of a valley filled with a perfect forest of timber. On both sides of the valley there are high mountains filled with precious minerals, dominated by 14,015-foot Sunshine Peak on the north. Crofutt described the area as "The almighty dollar in its native home."

The greatest disadvantage endured by Sherman was the one that eventually proved to be its undoing. The town was located at a point where Cataract Creek, Cottonwood Creek, and the Lake Fork of the Gunnison River all meet. The spring runoff was always heavy and floods were commonplace. Once, near the turn of the century, residents constructed a huge dam over a hundred feet high. A spring cloudburst took it out and then the water started on Sherman again. Only rich mineral deposits could induce people to rebuild their homes again and again at such a place. What you see today still shows evidence of the floods. In winter the town was deserted.

The city fathers planned a fine community with alleys and broad streets but destruction by the elements held its peak population to about three hundred souls. One hotel, the Sherman House, provided for human wants. A general merchandise store tempted the residents to spend their money at home since it also had a bakery, butcher shop, and a full line of groceries.

At one time the song, "Home on the Range," was alleged to have been written at Sherman in a dirt-floor cabin on October 2, 1873. Subsequent research, however, seems to discredit the story and it now appears to have been penned that same year in Smith Center, Kansas.

Sherman was strictly a mining camp, with both placer and lode mines. Work on the placers was done on a nearby prospect ridge. The lodes produced gold, silver, copper, and lead. Greatest local producer was the Black Wonder, the dump of which is still visible below the scar on the hillside north of the town. The Black Wonder mill was in the town itself and yields from it assayed from fifty to two thousand dollars to the ton. Many of the ores were shipped to Lake City for reduction. The road was, and still is, an easy grade by way of Lake San Cristobal. Originally a toll road, a fare of $2.50 each way was charged the user.

The town is located sixteen miles southwest of Lake City. Except for a few spots requiring caution, State Highway 351 is safe for regular automobile traffic as far as Sherman. The varied beauties of this valley form a constant succession of surprises. From its beginning just beyond Lake San Cristobal to its end where we find the steep beginning of Cinnamon Pass, it is a prodigious art gallery, hung with some of the most beautiful works of nature. The ruins of the town actually are off the trail about fifty yards on another side trail to your left and near the stream. The site of Sherman has been used by the United States Forest Service as a beautiful campground for the past several years. A few tumbled-down cabins plus the rubble pile that was once the great Black Wonder mill are all that remain of Sherman's main street.*

---

* In this same area see also Burrows Park, Carson, and Whitecross.

48.

SNEFFELS

THIS WAS one of those unusual camps where the mines paid off from the start and produced both gold and silver. When the first strikes were made and the town came to life in the late 1870's, it was first regarded as a silver camp, but as the shafts were driven deeper into the hillside, traces of gold were encountered with increasing frequency. The Revenue tunnel was begun in 1884 to intercept the rich Virginius vein. Total cost of this three-thousand-foot-deep bore was $600,000, financed by the Thatcher brothers of nearby Ouray. The property has since been called the Revenue-Virginius and is actually located within the town itself, with the cabins clustered around its entrance. Nearby were seven additional mining properties, the Governor, Senator, Hidden Treasure, Yankee Boy, Humboldt, Ruby Trust, and Atlas, all of which produced well and added to the local prosperity. Their total production has been estimated at twenty-seven million dollars and some of it assayed out as high as forty thousand dollars a ton.

During its boom, 1881 to 1919, the population of Sneffels hovered around three hundred persons. As with many other high-altitude camps, Sneffels was not worked as assiduously in winter though it was rarely, if ever, completely deserted during the snows. At some of the mines, workers often tunneled through deep snowdrifts to reach the shafts and work continued all winter long.

State Highway 361, a good dirt road, begins its long climb to the southwest, following Canyon Creek, out of

Ouray. It has been estimated that more tourists have been frightened into prolonged spells of descriptive universal adjectives on this particular stretch of highway than on any other in the state. It gains altitude fast and will require second or low gear most of the way up to the great Camp Bird Mine which made Tom Walsh a multimillionaire. It is a characteristic ledge road in the finest tradition with sheer, deep drop-offs and equally sheer rock walls rising up at the opposite side of the canyon. Though in reality wider than most such thoroughfares and quite safe, the absence of guardrails and the breathtaking surroundings create an optical illusion that causes many drivers to be apprehensive. In winter and spring, snow and rock slides have taken their toll of lives on this road over the years, and many stories are told about it locally. Distance to the Camp Bird is five miles. From this point, double back about fifty yards to the narrower trail that switches back up the mountainside to the west along more of the same ledge. About a quarter of a mile up, pull off at the overlook and stop for a good look at and pictures of the great Camp Bird layout, spread across the meadow directly below you. From this point, drive on for another three quarters of a mile to a cluster of buildings around a mine across the creek to your left. This is Sneffels. Cross the creek on the old wooden bridge to reach the town. The large structure was the boardinghouse. It should be noted that these buildings are not mere rude miners' cabins of chinked log construction. They were built of dressed lumber with expectations of permanence.

The town is built on one of the upper slopes of Mount Sneffels, named for the peak in Jules Verne's *Journey to the Center of the Earth*. Big spread-topped evergreens ring the meadow around the buildings and lean against the hillsides as though they were tired. It's a wild and shaggy-looking place but big, grand, and pretty, too. The rugged, domelike peak that raises its craggy summit behind the valley to the west is Stony Peak, lending an almost Swiss-alpine quality to the setting. The Ruby Trust can be seen by driving another mile up the road and the Yankee Boy is another mile or so beyond, where the road ends. A Jeep road goes west from the Ruby up to the Virginius. Don't try this one in your car. If you get up here, you will be provided with one of the finest vantage points obtainable for viewing or photographing St. Sophias needles without a telephoto lens.

Sneffels was started earlier than the Camp Bird and produced nearly as well. Except for its close proximity to the latter, it would probably have become the center of the district. Today, the Camp Bird is being operated by a British syndicate while the star of Sneffels has been eclipsed and its gaunt, sagging, buildings stand vacant.*

By 1980 the structures beside the trail had collapsed, but the rest were still intact as described.

---

* In this same area see also Ironton, Mineral Point, and Red Mountain Town.

Sneffels, located on a slope of the mountain of the same name.
The big boardinghouse is at the right center.

View of Sneffels taken from the dump of the Revenue Mine,
located above Camp Bird.

49.

TIN CUP

TIN CUP enjoyed the dubious distinction of being one of Colorado's three roughest towns. They once killed off seven town marshals in the short space of a few months. The Tin Cup mining district was thirty-six miles in length and twelve to fifteen miles in width. It was situated in the northeast corner of Gunnison County. In the past it had been essentially a silver mining camp, although considerable gold was found in all the ores. Near the end of the century some attention was given to prospecting for gold leads with marked success.

The town of Tin Cup lies at the south end of Taylor Park and is fourteen miles northwest of St. Elmo. By far the most colorful version of the story of Tin Cup's beginning fails to tally chronologically with the known facts and the account is reported here as legend. It has Tin Cup's story dating way back to the 1849 gold rush to California when a company of men from Georgia hired some civilized Cherokees to guide them through the Rocky Mountains. Near Tin Cup the Indians allegedly showed the white men enough gold to interest them but not to prevent their going on through to California, where they were unsuccessful in making a strike. Two years later, they camped on Willow Creek while on the way back home. Early the next morning, Charlie Gray stopped by the stream to get a drink, saw some likely-looking gravel, and rolled some of it into his tin cup and shook it. He was rewarded by getting a gold color. Excitedly he called to his companions,

who then began working with their own cups and soon
had some excellent gold-dust samples to show. Tin Cup
got its present name from these circumstances, though some
say it was Fred Lotts, Ben and Charlie Gray who were engaged in placer mining on West Willow Creek.

The other version of the story has it that they were hunting game when they discovered strong indications of gold
in a dry wash and took some of the dirt to their camp in
a tin cup such as prospectors attach to their belts. The
sample proved to be quite rich and gave the name to Tin
Cup Gulch, Tin Cup district, and Tin Cup camp, founded
later on March 2, 1879. In their excitement over the gold,
they failed to see that the buffalo had suddenly left the
park. When they did notice, it developed that a winter
storm was coming. The party started as fast as it could
go toward Granite but found it tough climbing the hill.
The blizzard caught them almost at the crest. They lost
several horses and barely reached the town with their lives.
Once in camp, they began making plans for a return trip
but, unknown to themselves, they were being kept under
strict surveillance by other men living at the camp. Every
move they made was carefully noted. Gray and Taylor
wanted to find another route by which they could get into
the park without being followed by the mob. Four local
men agreed to watch their every move. Jim Taylor caused
considerable consternation when he attempted to buy horses
to replace those that had been lost. Early in February,
Ben and Charlie Gray moved down below town and pre-
tended to be prospecting but knew they were being watched.
They purchased several horses from men who were will-
ing to sell at a price and moved on to Cache Creek.
When packed and ready, they went back to Granite and
paid excessive prices for additional horses plus a set of whip-
saws to cut the lumber for their sluice boxes. They returned to camp late that night and packed all their posses-
sions and started. They headed down the Arkansas for what

was then known as Brown's Camp. Nearby, they had been told, was a low pass to the south. After crossing and re-crossing the river in an effort to throw off any followers from their trail, they finally reached Brown's Camp in the present vicinity of Salida. Next they headed up Poncha Pass with a general idea of getting into the San Luis Valley. From the pass they went up Saguache Creek to Cochetopa Pass, where they found good feed and no snow. They wisely avoided the government agency at Los Pinos. On the west-ern side of the pass they found many drifts of solid snow and pushed on down to Tomichi. (Again the story seems unlikely since Tomichi was not founded until some time later.) Here they began to study the mountains in an effort to locate some landmark they might have seen from the park. They started up Quartz Creek and followed it as far as the forks, where it began to snow. After two days they discovered the snow crust and from this point they could recognize the landmarks of Taylor Park. The next morning, with packs on their backs, they walked over the pass and into Tin Cup Gulch. Timber was cut and fires were built to melt the snow. When they first reached the gulch, they found six feet of snow there. By the middle of April their cabins were built and they began to whipsaw lumber for sluice boxes, but it was the fifteenth of May before the water began to flow. The camp was on the lower side of Gold Hill where the water pitches over and begins to run down Willow Creek.

When the Taylor party left Granite, its absence was not noticed for two days. The four men who had determined to watch them immediately packed up and followed their trail to Chalk Creek where they were uncertain until they met a trapper who had been curious about Taylor's party and knew they had gone to the San Luis Valley. They pushed on and overtook Taylor on the Parlin Flats and had to hide until he pushed on. The Granite men followed the party up Quartz Creek and then up Gold Creek to the place where the first party had laid down blankets to get the horses across the ice. At Dutch Flats they made camp to wait and watch. They were caught in the same storm that had hit the first group and suffered severely. The following day they broke the snow crust into Union Park and, having gold pans with them, began prospecting and were rewarded with good color in the first pan. They took this back with them over the hills. The next year the town had its boom with several hundred miners, gamblers, and hangers-on gathering there. It became one of the richest gold camps in western Colorado. For a time it was called Virginia City, after a similarly named camp in Nevada. It was incorporated August 12, 1880, as Virginia City; but townsmen didn't like the name and on July 24, 1882, they changed the name back to Tin Cup. Out of one hundred votes polled, only three were cast against the change.

A man named Hillerton proposed to build a town and a smelter a mile north of the present site of Tin Cup. Later, sawmills were set up as they hoped to get some logs and keep sawing part of the winter.

When word of the discovery hit Gunnison, thirty-five miles to the southwest, the rush was on. By 1879, several hundred people were here and had hacked out cabins. There were plenty of saloons. The main street was called Grand Avenue. Washington Street crosses Grand and leads up to Mirror Lake. Most of the saloons were on this latter road. Peak population was about six hundred, all engaged in mining either directly or indirectly. There were twelve stores and shops of all kinds. Tin Cup had several hotels, chief among which were the Pacific and the Eagle. There were many saloons and billiard parlors as well. The most outstanding was Peroult and Company, better known as Frenchy's. After the summer of 1879, Tin Cup was rated as the largest town in Gunnison County, next to Gunnison itself.

The years 1880-81 marked the continuation of the boom.

One of the leading merchants, C. A. Freeman, carried a full line of groceries and kept a large burro train ready to deliver supplies on short notice. Delivery charge was 10 cents if it could be made in one day. One of his burros was the favorite of all the children in town because it could be ridden double or triple. After they were mounted, the burro would go from one tin can pile to another about the town regardless of the wishes of his youthful riders. He was called Old Croppy because at some time in the past his ears had frozen and they drooped mournfully from one side of his head.

There were three physicians in the town. One of them was Dr. McGowan, who always wore a full beard which resulted in his death while he was smoking in bed.

It was customary for the mines to close between Christmas and New Year's for the annual Christmas dance which was the main social event of the year. The men appeared in stiff shirts and tails. There was always a shortage of women partners since single women were not numerous.

With six feet of snow on the ground, the children always went to school on their skis, which stood outside the school in pairs. It was easy to count the school attendance in that way.

By the spring of 1882, the Denver and South Park hoped to reach Tin Cup with railroad service, but it failed to achieve its objective and St. Elmo was the nearest railroad point. No railroad ever served Tin Cup. In the summertime you rode the stagecoach and in the winter you skied. A railroad tunnel was started at one time under Tin Cup Pass but was not completed. Its remains are still visible above timberline, near the top of the pass on the St. Elmo side.

In the old days, Tin Cup was entered mainly from St. Elmo, over the old Tin Cup Pass, and frequently by way of Pitkin, Cottonwood, and Aspen. It was a rough trip from Tin Cup over the divide to St. Elmo in the early days. In the few warm months of the winter when snow was only four feet deep in Tin Cup and twenty feet deep on the pass, the way to get to St. Elmo was on skis. Each man was equipped with two large sacks strapped to his back as he climbed slowly over the seven miles, followed by the swift descent for the same distance on the other side. The trip was worthwhile in the winter because you could sell flour for $15 per one hundred pounds and eggs at $1 a dozen.

On the afternoon of August 15, 1906, the town of Tin Cup was razed by fire, typical enemy of every early mining camp. The town made an effort to rebuild itself but was never quite the same again. The fishermen who now tread the dirt streets of Tin Cup in their misshapen boots are not the lusty kind who killed the nights in Frenchy's in the days when men fought for what they got.

Tin Cup is located at the south end of Taylor Park, pleasantly situated at the foot of the continental range in one of the prettiest spots in the Rocky Mountains. Some of the loftiest peaks of the Saguache Range stand guard over the little hamlet. Four possible roads will take you there. Take State Highway 135 north from Gunnison. At Almont, turn right and follow the Gunnison River around past the Taylor Park Reservoir, where the road turns south to Tin Cup. A second road may be followed north from Parlin, through Ohio City and Pitkin, over 12,015-foot-high Cumberland Pass to Tin Cup, just barely beyond the foot of the pass. A third, and much shorter, but far more thrilling ride is the Jeep road across the ridge from St. Elmo. Up until just a few years ago, this was a real hair-raiser. Today it has been bladed out from St. Elmo to the top and is passable for any vehicle. However, from the top down into Tin Cup it is still a Jeep road, quite steep in places, paved with sizeable rock outcroppings in others, while a few streams and swampy places make the trail just difficult enough to be interesting.

Tin Cup Pass crosses the Continental Divide at an altitude slightly greater than twelve thousand feet and has been closed to normal highway traffic for more than a decade. Today, during July and August, Tin Cup has a local population of around two hundred persons, mostly tourists, fishermen, and a few semipermanent residents.*

* In this same area see also Hancock, Quartz, Romley, St. Elmo, and Woodstock.

Collection of Fred and Jo Mozzulla
This view looks north on Tomichi's Broadway and matches the picture on page 209

*Tin Cup, the town with the picturesque name, at the foot of
Tin Cup Pass in Taylor Park.*

*The completely obliterated site of Tomichi. Only the outlines of a few foundations,
at the left from the Jeep, can still be seen.*

50.

TOMICHI

Tomichi is another of those towns that has completely disappeared. It is currently identifiable only by comparison of the unm stakable contours of surrounding mountains which, of course, have not changed since the early photographs were made. Once the site has been found, careful and meticulous scrutiny reveals outlines of a few foundations along the west side of Broadway, which was the main street. On the northwest slope, barely beyond the town, the stone work of the Magna Charta Tunnel is still visible. This desolation seems in stark contrast with the Tomichi of 1880 which had a population in excess of 1,500 and boasted of being larger than nearby Whitepine.

In the beginning, the name of Argenta was adopted. A smelter was erected and operated until it burned down three years later. Ill fortune also dogged the bank and assay office, which eventually moved to another camp. Even the newspaper, the *Tomichi Herald,* had its share of bad luck and was printed on wrapping paper when inclement weather prevented the needed foolscap from reaching the presses. Another stroke of misfortune came just as the town was booming in 1893. When the silver crash came that year, it caused complete abandonment of the camp. A few prospectors defied the jinx to return to their properties in '96 and things picked up somewhat for a time until the final blow fell in 1899, branding Tomichi forever as a hard-luck camp.

A terrible rock-bearing snowslide devolved upon the camp,

carrying away the surface buildings and destroying the mining machinery. Some say five people lost their lives and others claim it was six. The snowslide added the final coup de grace and wrote finis to the life of Tomichi.

Easiest route to the site is a dirt road that leaves U.S. 50 just east of Sargents and runs north for six miles to an intersection where another road cuts across it. Cross this road and continue on north for an additional five mile to Whitepine. Follow the main street straight through Whitepine and beyond for another two miles and you're at Tomichi. The road is good for conventional vehicles as far as Whitepine, but a Jeep is recommended beyond that point as the old log bridges have deep drop-offs at both ends where it is necessary to ford the creeks. The boulder-strewn meadow inclining slightly to the west was Tomichi. The large rocks are still there from the big snowslide.*

The town was unchanged in 1980, but some new recreational homes have been built in the valley.

---

* In this same area see also North Star and Whitepine.

51.

VICKSBURG

VICKSBURG is one of our most accessible ghost towns. The road is a good one and turns west at the Clear Creek Reservoir, just south of Granite on U.S. 24, the main highway between Leadville and Buena Vista. The grades are easy and when autumn's chill turns the fragile aspen to a brilliant yellow-gold, the road is transformed into an aspen aisle to a point well beyond the town, providing almost unparalleled vistas for the camera enthusiast.

In one sense, it's unfair to refer to Vicksburg as a ghost town since summer residents from Colorado Springs and elsewhere have transformed the old miners' cabins, that line the one main street, into fine summer homes that still retain much of their quaint originality. Consequently, Vicksburg today, except for automobiles parked at the hitching rails, is not too different in appearance from the Vicksburg of 1880 when precious metals brought hordes from the States to wrest their fortunes from the nearby hillsides. Among the argonauts were many former Confederate soldiers who brought the name of the new settlement with them, calling it after the site of the battle between Northern and Southern troops in 1863 and more probably for the nearby town on the Mississippi River.

A second version of the story has the town being named for Mr. Vick Keller, of Keller, Peck and Company, who platted the town.

The first mining activity on Clear Creek was carried out in the interests of former Governor John Evans and

William N. Byers, founder of the *Rocky Mountain News,*
Colorado's first newspaper. In 1867 these two men established and later abandoned the La Plata mining district
along Clear Creek Gulch. During the summer of 1879
the creek bed was re-prospected and by Christmas there
were eighty-seven men in the district. Several valuable fissure veins were uncovered and the ores extracted assayed
at $112 to $244 to the ton. Between four hundred and six
hundred veins were ultimately uncovered. For a distance
of ten or twelve miles on either side of the gulch the sound
of blasting, picks, and drills could be heard. By October
of 1880 people were flocking in to secure claims, work and
to record assessments. The better known properties were
the Swiss Boy, Baracota, Ankland, Revenue, and Iron Cross.

In old records, location of the town was often described
as being in the Pine Creek mining district though some
call it the Clear Creek district. In either case it should not
be confused with the Pine Creek district above Clear Creek
in Gilpin County, which flourished in the 1890's.

In addition to mining, there were also several fine farms
in the valley. Lush grass grew well in the small parks
along the creek bed and in the higher valleys as well. Vicksburg was, and still is, accessible by a wagon road from the
mouth of the valley three miles below Granite on the Rio
Grande and South Park joint track, but no railroad ever
built up the creek bed to the town. The road goes up the
gulch for a distance of ten or twelve miles or as far as
Winfield at the head of Clear Creek.

At first the town had one store and seven cabins, with
about forty miners living in tents nearby while working
their claims. Later a blacksmith shop and additional stores
were opened to sell miners' supplies, liquor, and groceries.
Further successful business developments pointed to a permanent camp, open all winter with commodious quarters
erected, capable of withstanding the weather from November
through March. Many of the miners expressed a desire to

work through until spring. Even late in the season there was no abatement of the steady stream of prospectors going in, and none seemed to be going out except for supplies.

In 1881 a smelter was located four miles above the town, and a sawmill below Beaver was selling all the lumber it could produce. Additional evidence of prosperity was noted in January of 1881 when the Swiss Boy lode was sold to a Leadville man for two thousand dollars cash.

Eventually, as in most small mining camps, the veins pinched out and business began to close down. Little by little the population dwindled away until Vicksburg was deserted. Today, mining no longer plays a part in the economy of the town and its buildings are occupied only in summer.*

By 1980 more restoration had been done. A new road now goes around the south side of the town instead of passing through it.

---

* In this same area see also Gold Park, Holy Cross City, and Winfield.

The restored cabins along the shaded main street of Vicksburg

The main street of Waldorf. The large mill sits above its dump at the right center

52.

WALDORF

As FAR BACK As the early 1860's, visionary prospectors trudged up the alpine slopes of Mount McClellan. A few braved the hard winters and dug through the earth to a depth of several hundred feet. At this time the area was referred to as the East Argentine mining district. Although seeking gold at the time, the argonauts unearthed a large deposit of silver sulfide in 1867 and the story of Waldorf dates from that time.

Waldorf was a company mining town, the property of Edward John Wilcox who owned the Waldorf Consolidated Mining Company, sometimes referred to as the Waldorf Milling and Mining Company. By profession, Wilcox was an ordained Methodist minister. In later years this background was to provide some interesting and unusual aspects as it affected life and work around Waldorf.

When the town was built, it contained a large boarding-house, one hotel, a huge fifty-ton gravity-type mill which finally fell down three years ago, stables (which have since burned) for horses and mules, a machine shop, and a power-house. Its post office, which is still standing at this writing, was listed as the highest in the United State, built at an altitude of 11,666 feet above sea level. C. T. Tingle served in the dual capacity of postmaster and supervisor of Wilcox's mining properties, which produced about four million dollars' worth of silver, with smaller amounts of gold.

Roughly a half mile southwest of the town, the opening of the Argentine or Vidler tunnel is still visible. Originally it was planned to carry a railroad under the divide. If it had been completed it would have connected Leadville and Summit County directly with the Silver Plume and Georgetown areas.

At that time hopes were as rich as the mines. The only problem was a more efficient and dependable means of transporting ores and supplies between Waldorf and Silver Plume, nine miles away. With these factors in mind, Wilcox built the Argentine Central Railroad line in 1905-6 to serve his mines. It began operations on August 1, 1906, and was sometimes described as the highest railway in the world open for general traffic. He chose powerful little narrow-gauge Shay engines which made their way up from Silver Plume, switching back and forth across the sides of the high mountains before descending into the valley for the final climb into the Waldorf station. From there the train pulled up another two miles to the Santiago Mine for ore.

From Waldorf the tourist could take the hair-raising four-hour round trip to the end of the Argentine Central at the top of Mount McClellan, named for the general of Civil War fame. The stop on top lasted eighty-five minutes for snowball throwing, picture taking, or visits to the ice cave, a mine that was too solidly frozen for practical work. The beautiful ice crystals made it a fine tourist attraction and admission was charged. It was said that its walls were so solid that timbering was unnecessary. According to a 1909 timetable, the view from the top included about 106 peaks, counting some in Wyoming and Utah.

According to Mr. Edward B. Wilcox, of Denver, son of the founder, one of the engineers frequently admonished the tourists against stepping too close to the edge since the drop-off into Stevens Gulch is an extremely sheer and abrupt one. Invariably someone would timidly inquire if anyone had ever fallen off, whereupon the trainman would reply that a miner had stepped too close to the edge and dropped off "just the other day." When no further information was forthcoming, someone would shortly ask the inevitable question, "Did it kill him?" To this the engineer would crow triumphantly, "Naw, he had his rubber boots on and kept bouncing up and down for two days. We finally had to shoot him to keep him from starving to death."

There was a telephone line from the crest of the peak connecting the end of the line with Waldorf, for use in emergencies, and the trains always carried appropriate first-aid equipment. In later years, after the mines had closed and the steam trains no longer ran, an attempt was made to develop the route as a scenic attraction. In 1917-18, gasoline cars drove over the old grade to the top from Silver Plume and a fee of twenty-five cents was still charged to see the ice cave.

In 1907, while touring the European continent, Wilcox was offered three million dollars for his complete holdings in and around Waldorf. The offer was not accepted. At one time later owners of the road dreamed of extending this line from the top of Mount McClellan on around the crest of the ridge to reach Grays Peak, but this dream was never realized.

In recent years the road to Waldorf has become so well worn that even automobiles with shallow clearance may pass over it if moderate caution is exercised. Due to rather frequent articles and photographs published about it, Waldorf has become known as one of our more accessible ghost towns, easily reached in a round trip of a single day's duration to and from Denver.

The price of this notoriety has been vandalism. Three years ago, the huge old hotel and much of its original furniture went up in smoke. This past summer, the boarding-house was also burned, giving it the appearance of being one of our most forlorn ghost towns. Some camps have been mercifully reclaimed by pines and columbines while others have been destroyed by slides or hauled away. But the bones of Waldorf have been left to bleach on the slopes of Mount McClellan. At this altitude, the elements are harsh even in summer. Georgetown is three thousand feet below, Denver is fifty-five miles away and some six thousand feet lower.

To reach Waldorf, leave Georgetown on State Highway 281, a dirt-surfaced road that twists and switchbacks up Leavenworth Creek Canyon, finally passing above Green Lake. There are three intersections along the way and you should keep to the right at all three of them. In places the road is a ledge, cut through a profusion of quaking aspen that grow on the surrounding mountainsides. Above timberline you emerge into a long meadow. At its southwest end where the road starts to climb again is Waldorf, cinched down tightly to the side of the mountain. From Waldorf, the road through the center of the town goes across a creek and continues on, gaining altitude as it twists its solitary way to the top of Argentine Pass, which served as the main crossing of the divide before Loveland Pass was constructed. Here the road ends and is impassable, except for hikers, beyond the top. The narrow trail, cut from slide-rock, leads down to Peru and Chihuahua and the valley of the Snake River.

Leaving Waldorf in the opposite direction is the delightful drive over the abandoned bed of the Argentine Central Railroad to the top of Mount McClellan. A Jeep is recommended beyond Waldorf, but occasionally an automobile with fifteen- or sixteen-inch wheels reaches the top. This road is a dead end, too, but provides a superb view of Grays and Torreys peaks and a hiking trail for the hardy leaves this point and follows the crest of the divide over to Grays.

Waldorf was a lively place of few permanent inhabitants. Instead of hearing the lonely whistle of the Argentine Central, today's visitor hears only the creaking of Waldorf's ancient timbers. In 1980 Waldorf was a sad shell of its former self. Not much remains at the site now.

---

* In this same area see also Santiago.

53.

WALL STREET

VERY LITTLE but the stone wall remains today of the huge mill that was built in 1901 at Wall Street on Four Mile Creek above Boulder. Wall Street is located between Salina and Sunset on the dirt road that is known locally as the Switzerland Trail. The gulch had been laid out in town lots twenty-five feet wide for a distance of half a mile on both sides of the creek. A boardinghouse was built, also a two-story frame twenty- by forty-foot structure with a new addition of the same size. The town also included a general store and assay office. The stone building still standing below the mill was the company office and clubhouse for miners.

The completion and opening of the Colorado and Northwestern Railway, called the "Switzerland Trail of America," in 1898 was an event of great importance to Boulder County. The road ran between Boulder and Ward. Starting at Boulder, its route was westerly to the juncture of Boulder and Four Mile creeks, then in a northwesterly direction passing Crisman, Salina, Wall Street, Copper Rock, and Sunset. There the line divided with one branch going to Eldora and the other to Ward. On the Ward branch it took a detour and wound around up over the mountain, bearing west and then north till it reached Ward, thus passing by or near the most valuable mining claims in Boulder County.

In July of 1902, local crime reared its ugly head when the general store that housed the Wall Street post office was robbed. The proprietor and postmaster, E. B. Hall, noti-

fied the postal inspector's office in Denver but said that he
had not yet ascertained whether anything was taken from
the post office. From the lack of contemporary accounts,
it appears that no "ascertaining" was ever undertaken. True
to the noblest western tradition, the thief was soon caught
and turned out to be a young man who lived in the neighborhood. Later reports indicate that nearly all of the pur-
loined goods were recovered and the matter was settled.

The *Denver Times* of June 9, 1901, reported on the construction of the mill:

A $125,000 mill is emerging. The Wall Street Chlorination plant.
The process used is one introduced by John Greenewalt who stated that
$10.00 ore can be profitably treated. Capacity of the plant is 125 tons.

The Nancy Gold Mine Tunnel Company was organized
in 1902 to take over the Nancy Mining and Milling Company. The big mill brought prosperity to Wall Street for
several years but wasn't the success its backers hoped it would
be. The July, 1903, *Mining Reporter* mentioned that the
Nancy Gold Mine Tunnel Company was operating the mill
of the Wall Street Gold Extraction Company. The Last
Chance, Gray Copper, and the Gillard mines' ores were
delivered through the Nancy Tunnel. One of the best years
for the mill was 1903, but the area began to decline as the
ores ran out. Eventually the big mill was abandoned and
its machinery was hauled to Sugarloaf Mountain to the
south where it was installed in the United States Gold Corporation mill. The reasons for a shutdown are never too
clear and are rarely understood by the public it affects so
vitally.

Despite the loss of its mill, this was not the end of Wall
Street. The *Rocky Mountain News* of January 14, 1934,
carried this account of a renewed prosperity:

Wall Street is having a new boom. The little mining camp by that
name in Boulder County has eleven pupils in the school. A new grocery
store is opened and there isn't a cabin in the vicinity that's for rent.

Metal mining is the reason. Every mine in the Wall Street region is being worked, according to reports here and activity in nearby Salina and Crisman is picking up. A. H. Hindeman of Chicago is operating the Wood Mountain. A reduction furnace will be installed.

Inevitably, as in all Colorado mining camps, a decline finally set in.

The easiest of several roads to Wall Street leaves the Boulder Canyon road about a mile or so west of Boulder on State Highway 119. It turns north at an intersection marked Gold Hill and is paved for a short distance with a good dirt surface the rest of the way. At the next intersection, turn left and follow the road toward Sunset which will carry you into Wall Street. Today, very little remains of the original town except the great stone foundation walls of the mill, built against the side of the hill. A few cabins, occupied in the summer by people who work in nearby Boulder, and the schoolhouse are still there. The rest of the area has changed greatly and its former scars of civilization have been washed bare by successive years of thawing snow, leaving a townsite that little resembles its former self.*

Wall Street underwent a curious rebirth in the 1970's. It is currently reinhabited each summer by "street people."

---

* In this same area see also Gold Hill and Magnolia.

The chlorination mill foundation and some of the buildings at Wall Street

Some of the cabins, not original, at West Creek-Pemberton

54.

WEST CREEK

THIS SETTLEMENT was originally called Pemberton for Marsh Pemberton, one of a group of ranchmen occupying this beautiful upland valley about twenty-five miles north, in a straight line, and slightly west of Pikes Peak. In 1895 some slight evidence of gold deposits was reported in the valley and in an incredibly short time five hundred people were living in shacks and tents, frantically prospecting for gold.

Early in 1896 about five hundred square miles of public lands were thrown open to prospectors who were soon working the area east of where the town was later located. Several other small campsites—named Tyler, West Creek North, West Creek, North Creek, North Cripple Creek, Ackerman, and Given—were laid out. With little promising ore to be found, the miners held a meeting and planned to develop the best claims. Each man was to work a certain number of days for no pay with the understanding that he had no claim on the property worked unless minerals in paying quantities were found.

When the town was at its peak the main street was lined with buildings for several blocks. In May of 1896 two strikes were made. When the news had spread, men dashed across country to the site where a tunnel was being driven and the town laid out in 1897. Two women of Pemberton reaped a small fortune by baking bread and selling it for fifteen cents a loaf.

In later years the name of Pemberton was dropped and

the name West Creek was adopted to describe the whole area. A man named Hiram Abbey also laid out his ranch in town lots. He gave a site for the schoolhouse and donated land for the cemetery.

Life in such a place was often difficult, especially for infants and small children. Most of the people were transients, and often they were quite destitute.

West Creek is only partly a ghost town as people still live in the newer part of the community and a number of summer cabins dot the surrounding meadow. The valley is now occupied by ranchmen again, and some lumbering is being carried on at present.

State Highway 67 from either Sedalia or Woodland Park, west of Colorado Springs, will lead you to a short side road that makes a loop westward from the regular highway down into the sheltered meadow containing the town. A huge false front, now unoccupied, still stands near the store and dates from pioneer times. It is shown in most of the early photographs of the town. The woman who currently owns this structure is under considerable local pressure to raze the building, which the modern generation regards as unsightly and a firetrap. The owner is reluctant since, for her, the old building holds memories of her fiancé who made her a present of the structure back in the days when the community was far larger and more active than it is at present.*

By 1980 many of the older structures were gone. Some new construction is evident.

---

* In this same area see also Altman and Anaconda.

55

WHITECROSS

THIS TOWN can be difficult of access, depending on the condition, at any given time, of the ledge road above Sherman. The entire history of Whitecross has been colored by this very inaccessibility of the camp. Heavy snows arrive early and remain late in these extremely high mountain valleys. The difficulties associated with travel on and maintenance of roads under these conditions would be nearly insurmountable except for the motivation provided by the presence of rich silver deposits nearby in such mines as the Cracker Jack, Champion, and Tobasco.

In late June the snows recede, making the location of Whitecross a particularly beautiful one. The few dilapidated cabins that remain are laid out along one side of the narrow alpine valley. Across the trail from the cabins, the rocky slopes of Whitecross Mountain rise sheer above the valley floor. Adorning the face of an almost square knob of gray rock atop the mountain is a formation of white quartz in the shape of a cross, actually more of an X, that gave the town its name. The less elevated community of Burrows Park, at the lower end of the valley, once included Whitecross within its environs and the earliest records refer to the little hamlet as Burrows Park. The name was changed in 1882.

Mining development at Whitecross began somewhat later, in the early 1880's, than that of the surrounding silver camps which mushroomed in the San Juans during the middle seventies. It boomed again in the nineties and declined after repeal of the Sherman Silver Purchase Act. Sporadic activity continued into the present century, but weather that necessitated the annual abandonment of the camp during the long winters retarded development to the point where the peak population never exceeded a few hundred souls.

The huge expanse of the great Tobasco mill, built in 1901, may still be seen about a mile west of the town, stretching above the trail nearly to the top of the slope on which it was constructed. Its location is almost exactly at timberline.

Two possible trails, both more suited to hiking or Jeeps, are available to carry prospective visitors to Whitecross. Drive up State Highway 110, north of Silverton, through Howardsville, Middleton, and Eureka, following the canyon of the Animas River, to Animas Forks. At this point take the trail to the right, which is a Jeep road over Cinnamon Pass. A Forest Service marker indicates the location of Whitecross.

If you prefer, State Highway 351 out of Lake City becomes the Jeep road up Cinnamon Pass from the other side just past Sherman. Whitecross is beyond Burrows Park but before you reach the crest of the divide.*

---

* In this same area see also Burrows Park, Carson, and Sherman.

With people standing in the doorways of their cabins, George Beam made this picture of Whitecross.

After wading the Lake Fork of the Gunnison River, the author took this picture of empty Whitecross.

56.

WHITEPINE

THE HISTORY (or legend) of Whitepine dates back to the 1860's when two men allegedly discovered gold along Tomichi Creek and set about extracting it with crude sluices. In their anxiety to secure as much ore as possible, they failed to note the usual signs that herald the onset of winter. Remaining too late, they were caught in a blizzard, lost their sight, and eventually perished. This was the basis, sometimes elaborately embellished, for the legend of Snowblind Gulch. For years afterwards, prospectors sought Snowblind Gulch in their anxiety to follow and believe any will-o-the-wisp story that promised fast financial returns. Some credence was given to the tale in later years when remains of a sluice were found in the creek.

The initial strike, of which there is an actual record, was made in 1878 and incoming miners founded Whitepine as their residence center three years later. Although the legend had told of gold, the latter strike was silver and lead. The picturesque name was presumably chosen because of the great profusion of evergreen trees that still surround the town and are now beginning to encroach upon it. During the eighties Whitepine prospered and a population of about one hundred worked at the May Mazeppa mine, at the south end of town, and at several other good paying properties nearby. Two newspapers flourished during the life of the camp, but the most notable was the *White Pine Cone* which lasted for a decade and died with the town in 1893. Numerous stores served the human needs of the inhabitants and Sunday services were held in the schoolhouse. After the town was deserted, it lay dormant until the turn of the century. Following that, several attempts have been made to revive mining in the district but none approached the former success.

At present, Whitepine is occupied during the summer months by families who have converted a number of the more habitable cabins into fine summer homes. Winter snows, which often clogged the roads in pioneer times, still keep it from being inhabited on a year-round basis.

Drive north from U.S. Highway 50 just east of Sargents. This highway has no local number but goes north for eleven miles of good graded road to Whitepine. There were old signs at the only intersection, when last seen, which direct you to stay on the road straight north. The town is recognizable by its very long principal street, with assorted cabins and buildings of dressed lumber standing on both its sides. This town is much better preserved than most of those that shared the spotlight of Colorado's mining period.*

Much new construction at this site in the 1970's, making it difficult to identify the older homes. The road through town is now open only to foot traffic.

---

* In this same area see also North Star and Tomichi.

Upper main street of Whitepine, looking north up Tomichi Gulch

*Hotel and Tivoli Theatre at Whitepine. The small structure in the
foreground covered the town well.*

57.

THE WILD IRISHMAN

THE CAMP at the Wild Irishman Mine has been chosen for inclusion here as an example of one of the dozens of small mining communities that grew up around the many rich mines that once flourished in the high, remote, mountain country, located even farther back in the wilds than the regular mining towns.

The Wild Irishman camp is representative of a type of settlement where small numbers of men and their families lived and worked during the mining period. Any number of similar outposts could have been selected to typify this particular category, but I have two reasons for my choice. First, the Wild Irishman is sufficiently remote and therefore undiscovered by destructive vandals so that enough remains at the site to be worth seeing and is, therefore, worth the difficult trip in. Second, its geographical location, almost exactly at timberline on the upper reaches of Glacier Mountain, provides a particularly pleasing location and a few rewarding photographic possibilities.

Identification of these lesser known locations is not always easy. There is still an old map in existence that places a town called Rexford at this location. Another source of information identifies the camp as Preston, but both Mrs. Leland Sharp, of Montezuma, and the United States Geological Survey call it the Wild Irishman. It was a heavy producer of silver in the very late seventies, with its peak coming in the early eighties. It had no church or school and was never formally incorporated as a town, even though people once occupied the several cabins around the mine in order to be closer to their work.

The Wild Irishman is not easily reached by means other than a Jeep or by hiking. Start by following State Highway 294 from the foot of Loveland Pass (west side). Drive the six miles southeast to Montezuma. At the far edge of town, toward Webster Pass, take the two mile U.S. Forest Service trail up to Saints John and Grizzly Gulch. From the ghost town of Saints John there are three roads. The one at your left goes up to the several mine dumps on the hillside overlooking Saints John. The trail turning to your right is short and leads to another mine and scattered cabins among the timber. The middle one is reached by driving through Saints John Creek and across the middle of the town. There, half overgrown by willows and other low-lying shrubbery, are the tracks that indicate the beginning of the trail up to our destination. Drive about two miles; pass the first trail going off to the left—it leads to the Preston tunnel. The second left turn is the one you want and will lead you, without detours, to the Wild Irishman, a small miniature gem of a community with its few cabins lying in the timberline meadow in the shadow of the mine, which towers above the cabins at the far edge of the town.

If the day is warm and the sky is clear, you may wish to follow the trail that continues on through the camp and ultimately will put you on the very top of Glacier Mountain. In July, the mountaintop is covered with numerous species of small wild flowers typical of the Arctic Alpine life zone. From here it is possible to drive your Jeep across the tundra-covered saddle to the tops of one or two other nearby peaks or, if you prefer, just stay on Glacier and enjoy the breathtaking panorama of mighty snow-capped peaks that surround you from horizon to horizon. Don't forget your camera.*

---

* In this same area see also Montezuma and Saints John.

Timberline camp at the Wild Irishman Mine

Cabins, mine, and dump at the Wild Irishman, above Saints John on Glacier Mountain

58.

WINFIELD

SITUATED at the junction of the right and left forks of Clear Creek, where the streams come down and mingle together before going on to the Arkansas River, is the town of Winfield. In the early 1880's two prospectors pursued their runaway burros up the gulch into the far northwestern corner of Chaffe County. They ultimately caught them at a point about four miles from the top of the range. Before returning they stopped long enough to investigate some likely-looking specimens at the foot of Middle Mountain. The result was not the usual boom but a slow, sure, and steady progress. Five additional claims were staked out in nearby Mystery Gulch with several more in Gray Copper Gulch. The veins all showed gray copper, galena ores, and sulphurites that assayed well. A short time later the camp boasted of a post office, general store, two hotels, the inevitable pair of saloons, and the Silverdale Mining Company. One nearby claim was given a Spanish name *El Oro*, which was later changed to "El Toro" when it didn't pan out.

The closest railroad station was fifteen miles down below at Granite while Leadville was thirty-five miles away and Buena Vista was twenty-five miles south. From one end of Clear Creek to the other the hills were full of prospectors seeking claims for early development. Many continued work until late in the fall. Some effort was made to attract Eastern capitalists into coming out to look the camp over. There was an immediate need for machinery and a general optimism among the miners that there was enough ore to keep a half dozen concentrators at work day and night. Though only a small camp, production was estimated at between fifty and one hundred tons of ore per day for shipment.

The Union Redwood Company of Leadville finally erected a concentrating works at Winfield which operated successfully. Despite the many excellent properties in the camp, development was retarded by the miners not having the means to carry on continuous work. They were compelled to go out in the winter, when the camp was uninhabitable, and earn enough money for a grubstake to carry them through the next summer. Facing such conditions, it's not surprising that the camp lasted only three years.

The year 1901 saw a slight resumption of activity when a strike was made in the Tasmania tunnel. The mine was opened and the ore was in demand at the Leadville smelters. This late surge, however, was not sufficient to sustain life and Winfield was soon abandoned again, for the last time.

A number of log and slab-side cabins still stand among the high willows near the head of Clear Creek Gulch, south of Leadville. Though the road appears difficult in spots, a Jeep is not essential if caution is exercised. Follow the same instructions given for Vicksburg, continuing on through the town and up the gulch. Always stay on the trail that appears most used. Just below timberline in a mountain-ringed meadow are the several remains, including a false front, at Winfield. Close proximity to Clear Creek and easy access to superb mountain scenery make this a desirable camping spot and one or more tents will usually be found around the outskirts of the town.

If the day is sunny and the hour is early, you may wish to turn your Jeep and drive through the willows and across the creek. A few more miles up the rocky trail will put you at the old and now deserted town of Hamilton.*

---

* In this same area see also Gold Park, Holy Cross City, and Vicksburg.

The main street of beautifully located Winfield.
Note the typical false front at the right.

The roofless cabins at Woodstock, destroyed by a snowslide

59.

WOODSTOCK

THERE IS little left at Woodstock to mark the location of this small mining community in west-central Colorado.

Three possible routes may be followed to Woodstock. The first, over Williams Pass from Hancock, is one of the most perilous of the barely passable Jeep roads in the state, complete with a large and dangerous bog on the top of the pass. The trail is badly overgrown with willows and dotted with big boulders and steep grades. Woodstock lies just below the huge and historic Palisade of the Denver, South Park and Pacific Railway, above what used to be known as Sherrod Curve.

The second route is easier and far more desirable. Drive northeast from Pitkin toward Cumberland Pass to the point where the old railroad grade crosses Quartz Creek. Here it is necessary to ford the stream to get on the railroad bed from which the tracks were long ago torn out. I have twice seen conventional automobiles at Woodstock, though how they did it remains a mystery since the grade has high centers and washouts in several places. A sign marks the location of Woodstock.

The third route, Hancock Pass, is about equal in difficulty with the second. Like Williams Pass, it, too, leaves Hancock, crossing the divide in a series of occasionally steep but generally easy switchbacks. At the top, where the trails divide, go left down into the valley. The little cluster of cabins at your left was the town of Sherrod. The slash above it that winds around the peak across the valley was an above-timberline trail to Tomichi, which lies temptingly close, being at the head of the next valley immediately on the opposite side of the range. Rock slides, however, have made this route impassable.

Turn right from Sherrod and the trail will carry you another mile or so downhill to the three roofless log cabins of Woodstock, nestled deep in a grove of evergreens. The rest of the town is gone. The reason for this scarcity of evidence of habitation is included in the only information I have ever seen about Woodstock. It involves a disastrous snowslide which swept down the slope of the mountain above the town and ripped through the settlement in March of 1884. Woodstock was demolished and fourteen of the seventeen inhabitants lost their lives. Five children are said to have been among the fourteen. The town never recovered and was deserted.*

---

* In this same area see also Hancock, Quartz, Romley, St. Elmo, and Tin Cup.

INDEX